D1521260

THREE YEARS WITH WALLACE'S ZOUAVES

THOMAS WISE DURHAM

THREE YEARS WITH WALLACE'S ZOUAVES

THE CIVIL WAR MEMOIRS OF THOMAS WISE DURHAM

Edited by Jeffrey L. Patrick

Mercer University Press • Macon

ISBN 0-86554-822-6
MUP/H623

© 2003 Mercer University Press
6316 Peake Road
Macon, Georgia 31210-3960
All rights reserved

First Edition.

Book design by Mary-Frances Burt

∞The paper used in this publication meets the minimum requirements
of American National Standard for Information Sciences—Permanence of Paper
for Printed Library Materials, ANSI Z39.48-1992.

Library of Congress Cataloging-in-Publication Data

Durham, Thomas W. (Thomas Wise), b. 1840.
Three years with Wallace's Zouaves : the Civil War memoirs of Thomas Wise
Durham / edited by Jeffery L. Patrick.— 1st ed.
p. cm.
Includes bibliographical references and index.
ISBN 0-86554-822-6 (hardcover : alk. paper)
1. Durham, Thomas W. (Thomas Wise), b. 1848. 2. United States. Army.
Indiana Infantry Regiment, 11th (1861-1865) 3. Indiana History—Civil War,
1861-1865—Personal narratives. 4. Indiana—History—Civil War, 1861-1865
—Regimental histories. 5. United States—History—Civil War, 1861-1865—
Personal narratives. 6. United States—History—Civil War, 1861-1865—
Regimental histories. 7. Southwest, Old—History—Civil War, 1861-1865—
Campaigns. 8. United States—History—Civil War,1861-1865—Campaigns.
9. Soldiers—Indiana—Biography. I. Patrick, Jeffery L., 1963- II. Title.
E506.5 11th .D867 2003
973.7'472'092—dc21

2003010711

TABLE OF CONTENTS

ACKNOWLEDGMENTS

A number of people and institutions deserve my thanks for helping guide Thomas Wise Durham's memoirs to publication. Lieutenant Colonel James R. H. Spears (USAR, retired), the foremost historian of the 11th Indiana, read the manuscript and suggested a number of important changes. Joann Spragg, historian of the Ben-Hur Museum (General Lew Wallace Study) in Crawfordsville, Indiana, patiently answered my many questions during a hectic summer visit, copied several pages of information, and offered kind words of encouragement. She is the true keeper of the legacy of Lewis Wallace. The helpful staff of the Local History Room of the Crawfordsville District Public Library directed me toward several useful items in that collection.

Dr. Earl J. Hess of Lincoln Memorial University, noted Civil War author and expert on the 12th Missouri Infantry, suggested possible leads regarding the Helena "riot" between that regiment and the 11th Indiana.

John R. Powell of Harpers Ferry National Historical Park provided facts about Harpers Ferry in 1861, John Brown, and John Cook, one of Brown's followers.

Fellow National Park Service historians Terrence J. Winschel, Brian K. McCutchen, and James Jobe of Vicksburg, the Midwest Regional Office, and Fort Donelson, respectively, opened their historical files to me, located material, and assisted me in every possible way.

My good friend and fellow scholar Kip Lindberg took time away from his own Civil War research to review the manuscript, and brought several issues to my attention. He also located important material at the National Archives.

Craig Dunn of Kokomo, Indiana, has assembled one of the finest private collections of Indiana Civil War soldier photographs. He graciously allowed me to reproduce his image of Thomas Wise Durham.

The Indiana War Memorial Commission, a wonderful organization working to preserve our military heritage, freely granted me the use of images in its collection as well.

Finally, I would like to thank the members of my family, who were always ready to offer words of support and constructive criticism. By now they know a proud old Hoosier Zouave named Thomas Durham almost as well as I do.

ILLUSTRATIONS

LEW WALLACE

The 11th Indiana's battle flag

The Eleventh Indiana Volunteers Swearing to
Remember Buena Vista, at Indianapolis, May, 1861

The Engagement at Romney, Va., June 11th, 1861. The 11th Indiana Zouaves, Colonel Lewis Wallace, crossing on the double quick, the bridge over the Potomac.

The Day After Romney, The 11th Indiana Zouaves,
Colonel Lewis Wallace, in Camp McGinnis, June 12th, 1861

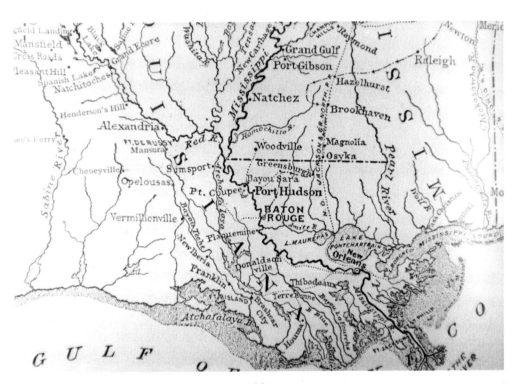

Louisiana

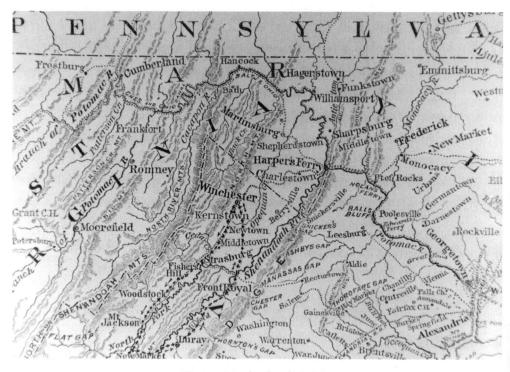

Western Maryland and Virginia

General Lewis Wallace and Staff, Zouave Regiment, 11th Indiana Volunteers

Charge of the Eighth Missouri and the Eleventh Indiana Regiments,
led by General Lewis Wallace, at Fort Donelson February 15th, 1862

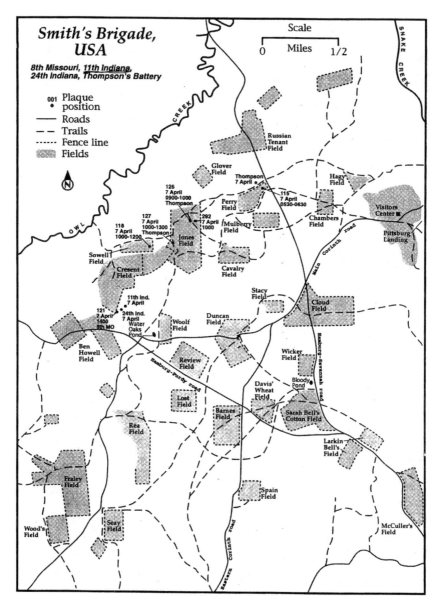

Positions of Smith's Brigade and the 11th Indiana during the Battle of Shiloh,
April 7, 1862. (Courtesy of Shiloh National Military Park)

INTRODUCTION

When the American Civil War began in April 1861, Thomas Wise Durham was an ordinary, twenty-one-year-old student and farmer's son in Montgomery County, Indiana. By 1864, Durham was a second lieutenant in Company G, Eleventh Indiana Volunteer Infantry, and a veteran of the battles of Fort Donelson, Shiloh, Champion Hill, and the siege of Vicksburg. When he resigned his commission and returned home to Montgomery County that summer, Durham formally ended his service with the Union Army. He never forgot those three turbulent years, however, and many years later, in 1911, he put pen to paper to preserve his impressions of life in the ranks of Abraham Lincoln's Hoosier volunteers.

Born 29 February 1840 near the small town of Waveland, Indiana, Thomas Wise Durham was the son of Jeremiah Brisco Durham. Jeremiah, a native of Kentucky, was a resident of Parke County, Indiana, when he purchased 80 acres of land in nearby Montgomery County in 1829. By 1860 Jeremiah Durham was a prosperous farmer in Brown Township, Montgomery County, with $8,400 in real estate and $4,030 in personal estate. His household included his wife, Minerva, six children, and a laborer boarding with the family.[1]

---

[1] Janet C. Cowen, *Crawfordsville, Indiana Land Entries, 1820–1830* (Indianapolis: self published, 1985) 136; Population Schedule, Eighth Census of the United States, 1860, Montgomery County IN, M653, roll 283, p. 37. Years after his death, Jeremiah Durham was described as a prominent farmer and stock raiser in Montgomery County, "a potent factor in politics," and "firm in his adherence to Republican principles." His wife Minerva was remembered as "a lady of great literary ability" (Chapman Brothers, *Portrait and Biographical Record of Montgomery, Parke and Fountain Counties, Indiana* [Chicago: Chapman Bros., 1893] 568).

Little is known of Thomas Durham's early life on the farm, but it is reasonable to conclude that his early upbringing was similar to that of thousands of other young men in rural Indiana. In a preface to his memoirs, Durham described his childhood this way:

> ...I will sum the whole thing up by saying I was just a common 'backwoods' farmer boy, was raised very strict by my parents, had to work hard, had many hardships and disadvantages, was chuck full of mischief, never did anything dishonorable, would never allow a man or boy to run over me, which caused me to have a good many fights and was fortunate enough to never get licked.

In April 1861, with the firing on Fort Sumter in Charleston, South Carolina, Durham felt the pull of patriotism and the lure of excitement and joined Company G, Eleventh Indiana Infantry for three months. Led by the famous Lewis Wallace, Durham and his comrades in the Eleventh saw service in western Virginia and Maryland before being mustered out that August.

Not content to remain at home, Durham quickly reenlisted for three years in the reorganized Eleventh Indiana. Soon promoted to sergeant, the young Hoosier saw his first serious combat at the siege of Fort Donelson in February 1862.

Two months later, while leading a company of skirmishers on the second day of the Battle of Shiloh, Durham suffered a serious wound to his right hip from a Confederate shell fragment, and became, as he later claimed, the first man in the Eleventh Indiana wounded during the battle. Durham was taken to a boat on the nearby Tennessee River and eventually moved to a hospital in Evansville, Indiana. Following a brief furlough at home, he rejoined his unit in June 1862.

Durham and his regiment endured several months of relative inactivity, then joined Ulysses S. Grant's army and participated in the Vicksburg Campaign. Weeks of marching and fighting ensued, including the bloody Battle of Champion Hill, Mississippi, in May 1863, before Durham and his comrades reached Vicksburg and helped man the siege lines around the city. After the Confederates surrendered, the Federals targeted a rebel force at Jackson, Mississippi, and soon captured that city as well. Although General U. S. Grant believed his men deserved "the highest honors their country can award," Durham was probably content to be commissioned a second lieutenant that summer.[2]

Following a campaign on Louisiana's Bayou Teche in the fall of 1863, Lieutenant Durham reenlisted in the Eleventh "for three years or during the war." After a furlough back to Indiana, Durham decided that he had had enough of army life and needed to attend to business at home. He resigned his commission on 9 June 1864 and returned to Montgomery County, Indiana.

Durham married in 1869 and soon moved his new bride to Baxter Springs, Kansas. He lived there until the winter of 1872, then moved to Lead Hill, Arkansas, probably making a living as a miner. In 1874, Durham was off again, this time to Indianapolis, where he stayed until the early 1880s, employed as a clerk and a guard. By 1897 he was living in Topeka, Kansas, then made his final move to Los Angeles, California, some time between 1911 and 1922.

Although Durham fathered two sons, neither lived past the turn of the century. Fred H. Durham, born in 1873, died in 1899 while serving with the US Army in the Philippines, while Claude B. Durham, born in 1875, succumbed to typhoid fever in 1897.

---

[2] US War Department, *The War of the Rebellion: A Compilation of the Official Records of the Union and Confederate Armies* (Washington, DC: Government Printing Office, 1880–1901) ser. 1, vol. 24, pt. 1, p. 59.

Dorothy, an adopted daughter, may have been the reason why Durham and his wife moved to Los Angeles, as they were all living together by the early 1920s.

Durham lived just a few years in California, apparently as a farmer. As he grew older he suffered from heart failure and apoplexy strokes, impaired vision and hearing, and increased blood pressure. His condition was such that his doctor believed he required "constant vigilance."

The old soldier was admitted to the National Home for Disabled Volunteer Soldiers Pacific Branch in Sawtelle, California, on 27 August 1925. At 1:15 A.M. the following day, Durham died from chronic myocarditis and arteriosclerosis. He was buried in Los Angeles.[3]

In 1911, Durham decided to record his Civil War memoirs for his nieces and nephews in Washington State. In a letter to his nephew, Durham explained the reason behind his book:

> I have tried to portray the joys and pleasures and sorrows, hardships and sufferings of a soldier in that war. You children know nothing of it only through history, and that does not give any of the little incidents of camp life. I have tried to give you an idea of the every day life of the soldier that you cannot get from history. I have given an account of some incidents that perhaps would not seem proper in a Sunday school or church paper, but if left out would not show life just as it was.[4]

---

[3] Thomas W. Durham pension record, RG 15, National Archives and Records Administration, Washington, DC. Durham's death certificate states that he was admitted to the Soldiers Home [Sawtelle CA] on 15 August 1925. Certificate of Death for Thomas W. Durham, State of California Department of Health Services.

[4] The version of Durham's memoirs used here is one typed by John H. Waugh, Durham's grandnephew, in 1929 using the original manuscript. The typed version is now in the possession of the editor. Durham's original manuscript has apparently been lost. An extensive genealogy of the Durham family that accompanied the typed version has been omitted here.

Like many other veterans of the Civil War, Thomas Wise Durham felt that the sacrifices of his generation needed to be preserved so that future Americans would know the enormous cost of saving the Union. Today many of these memoirs and reminiscences have been published, enriching our portrait of the Union soldier and adding a human dimension to our country's most terrible conflict. What makes Durham's memoir unique is that he faithfully recorded his life as both an enlisted man and a company officer during a number of important western campaigns (Donelson, Shiloh, and Vicksburg, among others). Although he intended the memoir to remain unpublished and read only by family members, Durham seemed to avoid exaggerating his role in the events he described. He did make minor mistakes as he struggled to recall dates and names from fifty years before, but he wrote with honesty and impartiality, recording incidents in camp and on the battlefield as he remembered them. Overall, Thomas Wise Durham's authentic account by a "common" soldier stands as a significant contribution to the genre of post-Civil War memoirs.

THE 11TH INDIANA VOLUNTEER INFANTRY

On 15 April 1861, President Abraham Lincoln faced two grim challenges: first, the United States garrison at Fort Sumter in Charleston Harbor had been attacked by South Carolina forces, and second, a new Confederate States of America had been formed to fight for the independence of seven Southern states. That day, Lincoln called for 75,000 troops to serve for three months to help crush the Confederacy and end the rebellion. The patriotic and enthusiastic citizens of Indiana rapidly recruited dozens of infantry companies under this call and sent them to Camp Morton, the state training camp in Indianapolis. There, before the end of April, ten of these companies were formed into the 11th Indiana Volunteer Infantry.

Commanded by Lewis Wallace, a Crawfordsville, Indiana, attorney, Mexican War veteran, and state adjutant general, the regiment was composed of companies from towns and rural areas in the central and west-central portions of Indiana. Students, farmers, and shopkeepers found their way into the 11th, although according to David Stevenson, librarian of Indiana, "Its ranks were filled with young men of the highest social position in their respective communities." Several companies were actually pre-war militia units, containing men who had received some military training, were disciplined, and were familiar with firearms. These included the National Guards, City Greys, and Independent Zouaves of Indianapolis; the Vigo Guards and Harrison . Guards of Terre Haute; and the Montgomery Guards of Crawfordsville. Added to this group were the newly recruited companies of Tipton's Rumsey Guards, the Wallace Guards (recruited from men at Camp Morton), the Indianapolis Zouaves, and the Ladoga Blues from Montgomery County. The latter became Company G of the regiment. One of its members was Thomas Wise Durham, a young student and farmer from Waveland, Indiana.

Lew Wallace's intention was to create a well-disciplined and motivated fighting force from this mass of citizen-soldiers. His experienced officers quickly began this process with frequent instruction in the Zouave drill. The camp schedule Wallace established called for reveille at 5 A.M., company drill at 9, battalion drill at 2:30 P.M., and taps at 10, with fatigue call, officer's drill, and dress parade filling the remainder of the day.[1] "It is enough to say," wrote librarian David Stevenson, "that the discipline adopted in the 11th regiment was more systematic and rigidly adhered to than in any regiment that ever left the state." An Indianapolis newspaper reported that "Colonel Wallace spares no time or labor in impressing his men with the necessity of discipline, and a thorough knowledge of military maneuvers."[2] In addition, Wallace contracted for a distinctive gray Zouave uniform for his troops in order to build esprit de corps. These unusual uniforms, loosely copied from those worn by the famous Zouave regiments of the French Army, were uncommon among Indiana soldiers, and further set Wallace's men apart from the other volunteers.

After receiving two flags on the Indiana state capitol grounds in early May, the men of the 11th Indiana were given marching orders. To the disgust of the young recruits, they were not sent to western Virginia, where combat was likely, but instead to Evansville, Indiana,

---

[1] *Indianapolis* (IN) *Daily Journal,* 26 April 1861.
[2] *Indianapolis Daily Journal,* 7 May 1861.

on the Ohio River. There "Wallace's Zouaves" were charged with stopping the contraband trade down the river as valuable goods moved from Northern cities to the Confederacy. The Hoosiers were joined by some artillerymen with two cannon, and together they stopped every "raft, barge, or steamer," searched the vessels, and seized any questionable items. In one instance, the men used their "saucy brass six-pounder" to halt the "Dunbar," a mail-boat traveling between Paducah, Kentucky, and Evansville. The captain of the boat vowed he would never "round to" for Federal troops, but when a blank cartridge was fired in front of the ship, the "Dunbar" came quickly to shore, with the Federal flag flying at her bow, amid the cheers of the whole regiment. After a close examination, the boat was allowed to proceed. Following the "Dunbar" incident, several other boats "visited" the Hoosiers as well, although they were not entirely voluntary visits.[3]

Despite the opportunity to use artillery against ships, the duty at Evansville proved to be less than glamorous for recruits anxious to "see the elephant" (the Civil War euphemism for experiencing combat). "We are anxious for a fight," one soldier warned, "and unless we have one…we will have a good deal of grumbling. We enlisted to fight not to lay around one place and another."[4]

The time spent in Evansville was not entirely unproductive, however. "There is no playing soldier now," wrote one Hoosier, "and the boys have to come up to the mark." "Every gun in the camp is kept loaded," he continued, "and the sentinels walk the beat with orders to shoot any one who attempt [sic] to cross the lines."[5] Another noted the increase in discipline since leaving Indianapolis, with several practice alarms staged to rouse the men from sleep and

[3] *Indianapolis Daily Journal,* 27 May 1861.
[4] *Indianapolis Daily Journal,* 20 May 1861.
[5] *Indianapolis Daily Journal,* 15 May 1861.

form them to meet an attack. On three occasions pickets actually fired at people lurking around the camp. "It is now no child's play," the soldier-correspondent cautioned.[6] "D.D.," another member of the regiment, believed that the presence of armed pickets convinced everyone that "we are brought up to the regular United States military discipline."[7] One Indianapolis newspaper believed later that the men returned from duty along the Ohio River with faces, necks, and hands bronzed by the sun and wind, with increased flesh, firmness, and strength of muscles in features and limbs. "An improved soldierly appearance was observed, and a renewed and strengthened confidence was felt in the regiment," said one observer, and everyone who saw the regiment agreed that the honor of Indiana could be safely committed to the trust of the 11th regiment.[8]

Fortunately for the volunteers, this river patrol duty did not last long. In early June, thanks to the intervention of Colonel Wallace, his men were ordered to leave Evansville and travel to Cumberland, Maryland. There they were to guard the critical Baltimore and Ohio Railroad line, which linked Washington, DC, with Wheeling, (West) Virginia, on the Ohio River. Once in Cumberland, Wallace was to report to his superior, Major General Robert Patterson, commander of the Department of Pennsylvania.[9]

The reassignment to Maryland thrilled Wallace's men, for a recent Union victory at Philippi, Virginia, the buildup of Federal forces in Washington, DC, and preparations for an offensive against

---

[6] *Indianapolis Daily Journal*, 20 May 1861.

[7] *Indianapolis Daily Journal*, 24 May 1861.

[8] *Indianapolis Daily Journal*, 8 June 1861.

[9] The main artery of the railroad (379 miles long) passed through Cumberland and linked Baltimore with Wheeling. An important connection to the Northwestern Virginia Railroad at Grafton allowed trains to travel to Parkersburg, on the Ohio River about 100 miles south of Wheeling, while a branch connected Baltimore and Washington (Festus P. Summers, *The Baltimore and Ohio in the Civil War* [New York: G.P. Putnam's Sons, 1939] 17–18).

the Confederate capital at Richmond had focused national attention on that theater of war. Despite efforts to send reinforcements to the region, the Union position in western Virginia and Maryland was far from secure. In addition to the large Union army in Washington, the Federals posted General Patterson in Chambersburg, Pennsylvania, and Indiana Brigadier General Thomas Morris at Grafton, Virginia. Wallace's 11th Regiment was assigned to Cumberland, about halfway between Grafton and Chambersburg. Facing the Union commands were sizeable Confederate forces at Harper's Ferry, Winchester, and Romney, Virginia.

As they rode the trains to Grafton, enthusiastic civilians in the towns through which they passed showered the new Hoosier recruits with cheers, tears, food, and mementos. When he arrived in Cumberland on 10 June, Wallace found that many of the citizens there also supported the Union cause. One of his men recorded that "Our regiment is very popular with the people here.... They do not look upon us as 'invading sacred soil,' but as welcome visitors and protectors."[10]

Soon after he reached Cumberland, Wallace received word that 1,200 Confederates were training at Romney, south of Cumberland. Rather than wait for the enemy to attack him, Wallace opted to take the offensive and throw the Confederates off guard. Not allowing his men to pitch their tents and rest in Cumberland, he resolved to move immediately with eight companies of the regiment. In addition, rather than take a direct and relatively short but predictable route to Romney, Wallace decided to take a Baltimore and Ohio train to New Creek, northwest of Romney, then use a difficult mountain road, hoping that his enemy would not fortify that approach to the town.

---

[10] *Crawfordsville* (IN) *Weekly Review*, 6 July 1861.

Early on the morning of 13 June, Wallace's Zouaves charged into Romney. Already warned that the Yankees were approaching, the Confederates took up defensive positions in a large brick house and held it for several minutes before the Hoosiers drove them off. Wallace then turned to face a battery of two guns and quickly forced the rebel artillerymen to flee as well. After searching the town for arms, camp equipage, and other military stores, the Indiana troops returned to Cumberland late that evening. Wallace's green soldiers had traveled an impressive 87 miles (46 on foot) in twenty-four hours, with no losses, and could claim that their first combat was a resounding success. Wallace proudly wrote, "My regiment behaved admirably, attacking coolly and in excellent order," and gave the locals "a wholesome respect for Northern prowess."[11] Union Commanding General Winfield Scott sent Wallace his congratulations, and even President Lincoln noticed the "splendid dash on Romney."[12]

Unfortunately, most members of the 11th spent the next several anxious weeks defending Cumberland without coming into contact with the enemy again. The only exception was a skirmish between thirteen of Wallace's mounted scouts and some Confederate cavalrymen at Kelley's Island on the Potomac River. After a vicious hand-to-hand struggle, the scouts were able to withdraw with light losses.[13] As they had done with the Romney action, victory-starved Northerners heralded the engagement as "one of the most heroic exploits that have occurred in the course of the campaign."[14]

Finally, on 7 July, Wallace was ordered to join Major General Patterson's command, now at Martinsburg, (West) Virginia, as part of

---

[11] US War Department, *The War of the Rebellion: A Compilation of the Official Records of the Union and Confederate Armies* (Washington, DC: Government Printing Office, 1880–1901) ser. 1, vol. 2, p. 124.

[12] Irving McKee, *"Ben-Hur" Wallace: The Life of General Lew Wallace* (Berkeley: University of California Press, 1947) 38.

[13] *Official Records*, ser. 1, vol. 2, pp. 134–35.

[14] McKee, *"Ben-Hur" Wallace*, 38.

an advance on the Confederate stronghold of Winchester. Soon after Wallace's arrival, on 15 July, Patterson's force moved to Bunker Hill, only a few miles from Winchester. All indications pointed to a major battle between Patterson and the town's defender, General Joseph E. Johnston, with the battle-tested Hoosiers sure to play an important role. "We will probably make an attack on thirty thousand Confederate troops who are entrenched only twenty miles from here with sixteen or eighteen pieces of artillery," wrote Hoosier S. S. Goldsberry. "We are going to tear things," he confidently predicted.[15] Another believed that "We shall probably…do some fighting on a large scale."[16]

If Wallace's soldiers had been led by a more aggressive general, their wish to see combat again might have been granted. Instead, the timid Patterson withdrew his force to Charlestown without bringing the Confederates to battle. No longer threatened by Patterson, Joseph Johnston left Winchester and traveled east by train to Manassas Junction. There he reinforced General P. G. T. Beauregard's army and played a key role in the Union defeat at the Battle of First Bull Run, just outside of Washington, DC, on 21 July. Having failed in his critical mission of holding or defeating Johnston, General Patterson marched on to Harper's Ferry and was honorably mustered out of the service a few days later.

The men of the 11th Indiana were no doubt deeply disappointed at the dismal end to the campaign. Despite his offer to keep his men in service an extra ten days in order to engage the Rebels, Wallace received word in Harper's Ferry that he was to leave the front and bring his troops to Indianapolis, as their ninety-day term of enlistment had expired. On 4 August 1861, the original "Indiana Zouaves"

[15] *Indianapolis Daily Journal*, 19 July 1861.
[16] *Indianapolis Daily Journal*, 4 July 1861.

were mustered out of service. Despite not having participated in any major battles, Wallace's men performed well in their three months of soldiering. They had displayed good discipline and courage under fire, and, in the words of Benjamin Harrison, "had not disappointed their friends at home." Indiana Governor Oliver Morton remarked that the Zouaves had "honored their State," "given Romney a place on the page of history," and remembered Buena Vista by wiping out the stain on Indiana's honor.[17] For Wallace, his actions in Maryland and western Virginia helped establish his reputation as a fighter and soon led to his promotion away from his beloved regiment.

The demise of the 11th Indiana in August 1861 was only temporary. Even before the regiment left western Virginia to return to Indianapolis, Wallace was given permission to reorganize the regiment for three years' service, recognizing the need for a more permanent Union Army. New recruits who were sworn into service as soon as they arrived in Indianapolis joined a number of veterans from the original unit, and by late August the reconstituted Zouaves were ready to take the field for extended service.[18]

This time, the Hoosiers were assigned to the western theater of war, but they would have to wait quite some time before seeing action again. The Zouaves arrived in St. Louis on 8 September and were immediately sent down the Mississippi to Paducah, Kentucky. With the exception of some minor scouting expeditions, the eager Indiana soldiers remained in Paducah through the winter, anxious to move against the enemy. "No fight—no signs of one," wrote one soldier,

---

[17] *Indianapolis Daily Journal*, 30 July 1861.

[18] Two Wallace biographers claim that only ten percent of the members of the original 11th Indiana reenlisted for further service. Wallace himself did not state how many men reenlisted, merely that "comparatively few" of the three months' men went to other commands (Robert E. Morsberger and Katharine M. Morsberger, *Lew Wallace: Militant Romantic* [New York: McGraw-Hill, 1980] 61; Lew Wallace, *An Autobiography*, vol. 1 [New York: Harper and Bros., 1906] 326–27). If we assume that the members of Company G were likely to reenlist in the same company, then a comparison of muster rolls reveals that only a handful of men signed on for further duty.

nicknamed "Snacks." "It appears to me that the gallant 11th will have to winter in this God-forsaken hole," he added. Such an arrangement galled many of Wallace's men, who were anxious to "return home 'covered with glory.'" Snacks was thankful that the regiment had already earned a reputation for fighting, for he thought the war was sure to end before the opening of spring and thus prevent them from seeing more combat.[19] It was not until February 1862 that a major winter campaign began against the Confederates in the West.

Wallace took advantage of the lull in Paducah to ready his men for the next clash with the enemy. "He never tires," wrote one Indiana man. The enthusiastic Wallace was said to neglect sleep, food, and "social converse" in favor of a battalion drill or dress parade. In addition, preparations were made to defend Paducah in case of a rebel attack. Wives and children of officers and soldiers were ordered away, and activities such as wood chopping and ditch digging occupied the troops, in order to make an enemy approach "as difficult and dangerous as possible."

Despite making forests vanish and hills appear where valleys existed before, many soldiers doubted that these "artificial arrangements" would be tested. "My chance of smelling gunpowder here is growing 'beautifully less' every day," wrote Snacks. "The rebels have got it into their heads that there is a trap laid here for their destruction."[20] Eventually, even the optimistic Wallace complained about the inactivity. In the words of one biographer, he "chafed...talked of resigning, and pulled wires to get transferred to another army."[21] By late December, however, one hopeful Zouave correspondent, not as optimistic about the end of the war, was "expecting every day to

---

[19] *Indianapolis Daily Journal,* 9 November 1861.

[20] *Indianapolis Daily Journal,* 24 October 1861.

[21] McKee, *"Ben-Hur" Wallace,* 41.

[22] *Indianapolis Daily Journal,* 28 December 1861.

receive orders to advance upon the stronghold of rebellion" and believed "Our regiment is now well prepared for a forward movement."[22]

Finally, the Hoosiers were ordered to leave Paducah, and when they marched out of town, they had four new commanders— Brigadier General Ulysses S. Grant commanded their army, Brigadier General Charles F. Smith headed their division, Colonel Wallace (now a brigadier general) led their brigade, and Colonel George F. McGinnis, formerly the unit's lieutenant colonel, rode at the head of the regiment.

The Indiana Zouaves sailed up the Tennessee River toward the targets of Forts Heiman and Henry. Once secured, Grant's army would then march overland twelve miles to capture Fort Donelson on the Cumberland River. The fall of the three forts would secure two major rivers that could then be used as invasion routes—the Tennessee all the way to the borders of Mississippi and Alabama, and the Cumberland to the Tennessee capital of Nashville.

As a Union naval flotilla bombarded Fort Henry into submission, the 11th Indiana marched down the opposite bank of the Tennessee River and found Fort Heiman deserted. By the evening of 6 February, two of the three forts Grant hoped to capture had fallen with little struggle. Unfortunately most of Fort Henry's garrison escaped to Donelson, so the effort to take that post would prove to be much more costly.

While the remainder of the army marched on Fort Donelson, the Hoosier 11th and the rest of General Wallace's brigade remained behind at Heiman to guard the recently won forts against any possible Confederate counterattack. Although disappointed, Wallace found his stay at Heiman a temporary one. On 13 February, Grant's army began to lay siege to Fort Donelson, and soon the commanding general sent a message to Wallace to bring his men and rejoin the army. The following morning, after making the overland march ("little more than a wholesome constitutional to a vigorous man," Wallace wrote in his autobiography), the young Indiana general found General Grant and the rest of the Federals outside Donelson.

Once he reported to Grant, Wallace was shocked to discover that he was to turn over command of his old brigade to Colonel Morgan L. Smith. Instead, Wallace was to take charge of several regiments designated the "Third Division" of Grant's army. The 11th Indiana and the remainder of Wallace's brigade were ordered to remain with General C. F. Smith's Second Division. Even though Lew Wallace was formally separated from his old comrades, the fortunes of war soon brought the Hoosiers together again on the field of battle.

The day Wallace arrived at Donelson, Grant hoped to achieve success against the Confederates by sending a gunboat flotilla down the river to pound the fort's water batteries into submission and then sail on into the Confederate rear. The combination of siege by land and sea would surely force Donelson's surrender. Instead, the rebel artillerymen put up a stout defense of the river, hammered the Federal ships, and forced them to withdraw.

Moreover, on the morning of 15 February, the Confederates launched a massive effort to break out of Fort Donelson and escape Grant's trap. The Federal right flank was pushed back, and by early afternoon the rebels had opened an escape route. Misunderstood orders and faulty communications in the Confederate ranks plus the arrival of Federal reinforcements soon turned the tide. Joined by his old 11th and other Federal regiments, Lew Wallace drove the rebels back inside their works and recovered the ground lost that morning. Facing less resistance as the Confederates shifted troops to support their breakout, Union regiments on Grant's left flank charged the enemy earthworks and actually captured part of the Confederate outer defenses.

The following day, Brigadier General Simon Buckner, the commander of the Donelson garrison, agreed to surrender terms. Although some rebels escaped, Grant bagged at least 15,000 prisoners. Fort Donelson was the first great Union victory in the West, and Lew Wallace (soon promoted to major general) and the Hoosiers of the 11th Indiana proved that the willingness to fight they had demonstrated at Romney in 1861 was still present many months later in an entirely different theater of war.[23]

Changes were in store for the 11th after the fall of Fort Donelson. Only a few days after the campaign ended, the regiment returned to Lew Wallace's command, joining his Third Division. In mid-March, Grant moved his men up the Tennessee as the initial step of an advance on the critical Southern rail junction of Corinth, Mississippi. The capture of Corinth would secure the Memphis and Charleston Railroad, a major Confederate east-west line, and the Mobile and Ohio, stretching north and south. While most of Grant's army was positioned near Pittsburg Landing, Wallace and his division were stationed in the vicinity of Crump's Landing, about six miles by land (four by water) to the north.

As Grant's men sat in camps near Pittsburg and Crump's Landings, a large Confederate army came together in Corinth and planned to strike the Federals a crippling blow. Few if any in the 11th Indiana's camp thought that they would hear shots fired in anger until they advanced on Corinth. Dan Macauley of the 11th thought his men would be enjoying "stationary activity" for some time to come, playing "'Home Guard' and 'chuck-luck' [sic] until further orders." He described a bucolic scene of trees in blossom, green fields, a glorious sky, camp after camp of soldiers, and "our victorious flags."

---

[23] One biographer has argued that although Wallace believed he had "saved the whole army," Generals Grant, Smith, and McClernand either briefly acknowledged his actions or failed to mention his role at all (McKee, *"Ben-Hur" Wallace*, 45).

[24] *Indianapolis Daily Journal*, 14 April 1862.

Rumors persisted that the Confederates were making every prepara-
tion for defending Corinth, not planning to take the offensive.[24]

The peaceful calm was shattered on the morning of 6 April, when
General Albert Sidney Johnston's Army of the Mississippi launched a
furious attack on the surprised Federal encampment. Throughout
the day, despite determined fighting, Grant's men were steadily
pushed back to Pittsburg Landing on the Tennessee River. The beleaguered Union commander desperately needed Lew Wallace's
5,800-man division to stem the Confederate advance, and although
Grant sent several couriers to urge Wallace to march with all possible
speed, he waited in vain for the Hoosier to arrive at the landing.

Although Wallace heard the fighting near Pittsburg Landing that
morning and called his men to attention, it was not until almost
noon that the general and his division received orders to begin the
six-mile march to the Shiloh battlefield. Unfortunately, they traveled
a prearranged route determined by Wallace before the battle, one that
would take them far to the west of Pittsburg Landing and to the
Union camps. This route would have been ideal if the camps had
been held against the Confederate onslaught, but was useless now
that the Federals had been driven back to the landing. Fortunately,
messengers from Grant found Wallace and explained that the River
Road to Pittsburg Landing would be the most direct route to reach
Grant. The Hoosier general retraced his steps, reached the River
Road, and finally brought his men to the landing after dark. What
should have been a short, quick march had taken seven hours and
covered fifteen miles. Wallace's tardy arrival caused him a great deal
of hardship during and after the war as he sought to defend his
actions on 6 April 1862.

Early on the morning of 7 April, Wallace's division was in position on the Federal right flank, ready to join in the effort to drive the
Confederates away from Pittsburg Landing. As the Federal skir-

mishers advanced, Confederate Colonel Preston Pond's brigade retired, covered by Ketchum's Alabama Battery. It was probably this battery that wounded Sergeant Thomas Wise Durham with a spherical case shot fragment, making him arguably the 11th's first casualty at Shiloh.

Wallace's division slowly but steadily pushed back the Confederate left, and by late afternoon had marched well beyond the other Federal units in pursuit of the retreating enemy. Unsupported in his advanced position, Wallace fell back and joined the rest of the army to camp for the night. In the single day of fighting his division suffered 296 casualties. Wallace was no doubt impressed by the fact that his old 11th Indiana suffered the highest casualties in the division. He paid tribute to all his men in his official report of the battle: "'Not one man, officer or soldier, flinched,'" he wrote, and "Ohio, Indiana, Missouri, and Nebraska will be proud of the steadfast Third Division, and so am I."[25] Their performance in the battle had a profound impact on the Hoosiers as well. Although General Wallace remembered the fight as "indescribably grand," a member of the 11th labeled the field of Shiloh as the place "where the earth drank the blood of slain thousands with a passionate thirst."[26]

Following the Battle of Shiloh, the Hoosiers advanced toward the rebel stronghold of Corinth, Mississippi. Along the way they enjoyed their first summer in the "Sunny South." "It was uncomfortably warm and the sun drove us into cover from ten to four o'clock every day," wrote one Indiana man. "Moreover, insects, bugs and reptiles of all sorts and sizes" made their appearance. To add to their woes, rebel cavalry and citizens would shoot or capture Federal soldiers who ventured too far outside their picket lines. Those who did explore the

[25] *Official Records*, ser. 1, vol. 10, p. 173.
[26] McKee, *Ben-Hur" Wallace*, 51; *Indianapolis Daily Journal*, 23 September 1862.

area found worthless soil, miserable log cabins, no fences, fields of grain trampled, and men and women half clad and "imperfectly developed, both mentally and physically," looked upon as objects of pity, not hatred.[27]

After the Confederates gave up Corinth without a fight, the 11th moved from the countryside to spend a brief and uneventful period in Memphis. There, although the 11th had performed well in two major battles, Wallace kept the men drilling to maintain their fighting edge, "and the dress parades of the Zouaves became the rage, thousands flocking to see them go through the exercises of their unique drill," according to one writer. Despite worn, soiled uniforms, their weapons were kept in "a perfect line of polished steel" as they moved like parts of a great machine in "a marvel of perfect drill."[28]

Sadly, in the summer of 1862 Wallace was granted a short leave of absence to attend to affairs at home. Then, primarily because of his delayed march to the Shiloh battlefield, he was relieved from command of his division. With this order, Wallace was permanently separated from his Hoosier comrades and forced to cheer his Zouaves from afar until war's end. Despite his successful organization of the defenses of Cincinnati in 1862 and his competent coordination of forces against Confederate raider John Hunt Morgan in Indiana the following year, Wallace had to wait until 1864 for his next significant command and recognition of his military abilities.[29]

In July 1862, orders came moving the regiment across the Mississippi to Helena, Arkansas. There the Hoosiers spent the next several months in camp, distressed because they were not involved in

---

[27] *Indianapolis Daily Journal*, 24 May 1862.

[28] *Indianapolis Daily Journal*, 1 July 1862.

[29] McKee, *"Ben-Hur" Wallace*, 53. An account of Wallace's defense of Cincinnati may be found in Vernon L. Volpe's "'Dispute Every Inch of Ground': Major General Lew Wallace Commands Cincinnati, September 1862," in the *Indiana Magazine of History* 85/2 (June 1989): 138–50.

active operations. "This veteran army of thirty thousand souls remains in idleness," grumbled one Hoosier. "If our army could degenerate into demoralization by inactivity," he added, the army in Helena would obscure its well-earned honors "by a sad state of degeneracy." Another believed that he was "doomed to a long stay in this lonely spot of the green earth," and thought it a shame that men who had won such a fine reputation "on two of the hardest fought fields of the war, should thus be left as a garrison." [30] A member of the regiment identified only as "H" disgustedly wrote, "we have done nothing for the government or for ourselves since the 'little brush' we had at Shiloh.... [We] are nearly ready to conclude that the fates have assigned us to this desolate, do-nothing hole, as a 'fixed institution.'"[31]

Relief from the boredom was provided when the Federals occasionally left the city on minor expeditions against Confederate forces in Arkansas. General Alvin P. Hovey, the Union commander in eastern Arkansas, frequently sent expeditions of cavalry and infantry up and down the river and into the country to discover the enemy's movements and disperse Confederate guerrilla bands.[32] In addition, "Picket skirmishing occurs almost daily and nightly," observed one soldier, as guards along the river sought to protect boats from the rebel guerrillas and "their evil work."[33] After a spring filled with the usual routine of drills and dress parades, the 11th Indiana was ready for another major campaign in 1863, one that would add several battle honors to their regimental colors.

With the coming of the new year, the 11th became part of the effort to capture the Confederate bastion of Vicksburg, Mississippi.

---

[30] *Indianapolis Daily Journal*, 31 October 1862.
[31] *Indianapolis Daily Journal*, 2 March 1863.
[32] *Indianapolis Daily Journal*, 18 November 1862.
[33] *Indianapolis Daily Journal*, 31 October 1862.

Again under the overall command of Ulysses S. Grant, the Hoosiers were assigned to General Alvin P. Hovey's Division of John A. McClernand's 13th Army Corps. In April 1863, the regiment traveled by boat to Miliken's Bend, Louisiana, northwest of Vicksburg. Disembarking there, the Hoosiers marched south to Hard Times Landing and waited to be transported across the Mississippi. In the meantime, a Union fleet ran south past the Vicksburg defenses, and in late April ferried the 13th Corps across the river to Bruinsburg, Mississippi.

Not far from the landing site, the Federals clashed with an outnumbered Confederate force at Port Gibson on 1 May. The 11th played a conspicuous part in driving the rebels from the field. Grant pushed his army to the northeast, avoiding a direct attack on Vicksburg. He planned instead to march on the railroad linking Vicksburg and Jackson, Mississippi, to cut that lifeline to the fortress city. As he approached the rail line, Grant turned to face Confederate reinforcements marshalling at Jackson. If he captured that city, he would disrupt the railroad line, scatter the rebels there, then be able turn east and move on Vicksburg, secure in the knowledge that no sizeable enemy force would attack his rear. After a short fight on 14 May, the Confederates evacuated Jackson and joined General Joseph E. Johnston, and the Union 15th and 17th Army Corps captured the city. With Jackson's fall, the 15th and McClernand's 13th Corps turned west toward Vicksburg.

Confederate Lieutenant General John C. Pemberton left Vicksburg with three divisions (about 23,000 men) and attempted to carry out General Johnston's orders to join him north of Jackson. But Pemberton's move came too late—Grant's advancing Federals brought him to battle on the morning of 16 May at Champion Hill, about halfway between Jackson and Vicksburg. The 11th Indiana was heavily engaged from the start of the action, first helping to push the

Confederates back, then being forced to retreat by a rebel counterattack. With the arrival of reinforcements, Grant's line held and by late afternoon Pemberton's army was in retreat. The Confederates withdrew to the Vicksburg defenses.

The Battle of Champion Hill was perhaps the most hard-fought action in the 11th Indiana's career, as more than 150 members (more than one-third) of the regiment became casualties during the seesaw fighting. Even Grant admitted that Hovey's men had fought bravely and bled freely to secure the victory.[34] General Hovey himself poetically wrote the following about his regiments in a report to Major General John McClernand: "They have won laurels on many fields, and not only their country will praise, but posterity be proud to claim kindred with the privates in their ranks."

Grant's army now closed in around the beleaguered city on the Mississippi. After two failed Union assaults (the 11th Indiana was not seriously engaged in either), the Union army began formal siege operations to take Vicksburg. The Indiana Zouaves endured a routine and laborious but potentially deadly stint in trenches surrounding the enemy. After a month and a half of siege work, Vicksburg fell on 4 July 1863. By the time of the Confederate surrender, Hovey's Division had lost only nineteen men killed and seventy-six wounded, but the Hoosier general praised the "great firmness, coolness, and bravery" of his men during the siege. Hovey was proud of the fact that for more than forty days they were "under constant fire, casualties happening daily in the midst of their camps…in their beds, at the table, in the rifle-pits, and yet…there was no murmur, no complaint."[35]

With the end of yet another triumphant Federal campaign, the men of the 11th hoped for a rest. Instead, the Zouaves received orders

---

[34] Ulysses S. Grant, "The Vicksburg Campaign," in Robert U. Johnson and C. C. Buel, *Battles and Leaders of the Civil War*, vol. 3 (New York: Thomas Yoseloff, 1956) 513.

[35] *Official Records*, ser. 1, vol. 24, pt. 2, pp. 45, 241.

to march to Jackson, Mississippi, to help General William T. Sherman deal with the large Confederate army under General Joseph Johnston. Johnston and his 32,000 Confederates had made tentative moves toward relieving Pemberton in Vicksburg, but Grant had kept careful watch on this potent force, and Johnston had made no serious attempt to aid the trapped rebels. Now with Pemberton's army gone, Grant was free to turn on Johnston, who had retreated to Jackson. Grant conducted a seven-day siege against Johnston, forcing the Confederate commander to evacuate his force on the night of 16 July. The Federals occupied the city again the following day.

Wallace's Zouaves were fortunate to participate in this final victory of the Vicksburg Campaign with a loss of only eleven men. Their commanders were proud of their actions during this siege as well, as Brigadier General Alvin Hovey noted [in his official report] that his division "was under a continual fire, and fully returned it." Colonel William Spicely, the 11th's brigade commander, wrote that his brigade had "a record for gallantry and bravery on every field of battle which words fail to describe. All honor to the men of the First Brigade."[36]

In July 1863, Union general-in-chief Henry W. Halleck proposed that Department of the Gulf commander General Nathaniel P. Banks establish a Federal presence in Texas. Banks's need for reinforcements to accomplish this goal led to the movement of the 13th Army Corps from Vicksburg and Natchez to Carrollton, Louisiana, the following month. The 11th remained in this suburb of New Orleans for only a few weeks, then was transported by rail to Brashear City, Louisiana. The Hoosiers moved on to Berwick, joining Banks's large force moving up the Bayou Teche, hoping to march overland through western Louisiana into Texas. Under the immediate command of

[36] Ibid., 546, 599–601.

General William B. Franklin, the 11th marched to Opelousas in late October, but faced with a lack of water and forage in the western portion of the state, Banks canceled the remainder of the march and Franklin's troops were ordered to New Iberia. Banks himself left the expedition and moved a portion of his forces to the Texas coast.

While Franklin's retreat was in progress, a large force of Confederates attacked one of his brigades on 3 November near Grand Coteau. After 200 members of the 67th Indiana were captured, the 11th and other Federal reinforcements arrived and drove the enemy away. Franklin's men finished their withdrawal to New Iberia, some 100 miles west of New Orleans. Although the Hoosiers and their comrades had done a great deal of marching, the Banks/Franklin expedition had accomplished nothing. The 11th Indiana moved on to Algiers and on 15 January 1864 was assigned to duty in the defenses of New Orleans. The Hoosiers then marched to Madisonville, north of the city, and awaited further orders.[37]

In late February, those men in the 11th who reenlisted for three years or the duration of the war were granted furloughs home, and, after sailing to New York City, arrived in Indianapolis on 22 March 1864. There they turned in their arms and accoutrements, and, "free from military restraint, they all enjoyed themselves finely" during the thirty-day furlough. On 29 April, the veterans of the 11th Indiana reassembled, drew their weapons, and prepared to return to the war.[38]

The regiment moved to New Orleans, then back to Carrollton, where it remained until late May, having been fortunate enough to miss General Banks's disastrous Red River Campaign against Shreveport that spring. After duty in Thibodeaux and Algiers,

---

[37] An excellent concise account of the Bayou Teche operation may be found in Frank J. Welcher, *The Union Army 1861–1865*, vol. 2 (Bloomington: Indiana University Press, 1993) 56–57.
[38] Theodore T. Scribner, *Indiana's Roll of Honor* (Indianapolis: A. D. Streight, 1866) 278.

Louisiana, the Hoosiers received sealed orders taking them away from the western theater for the duration of the war.

The 11th Indiana sailed to Washington, DC, joined the 19th Army Corps, and participated in Major General Philip Sheridan's campaign against Jubal Early in the Shenandoah Valley. The regiment was conspicuously involved in the dramatic Union victories at the Battles of Winchester, Virginia, on 19 September, Fisher's Hill three days later, and Cedar Creek on 19 October. Once again, the Hoosiers garnered accolades from their superior officers for their excellent conduct, and suffered more than 125 total casualties in the three actions. Two of them won the Medal of Honor for heroism at Winchester.

The 11th spent the spring of 1865 in Baltimore and was finally mustered out of service in July. The following month the Hoosiers returned to Indianapolis, where they were received by Governor Morton, and were officially discharged a few days later. "Wallace's Zouaves" compiled an impressive combat record during the Civil War. Although the three-month regiment fought in only minor skirmishes in western Virginia in the summer of 1861, the reorganized 11th Indiana participated in some of the bloodiest and most important battles and campaigns of the Civil War, from Fort Donelson, Shiloh, and Vicksburg to the Shenandoah Valley. The Zouaves marched more than 9,000 miles, served in three different armies and eight different states, and suffered 288 total losses.[39]

Although scarcely remembered today, Thomas Wise Durham and his comrades in the ranks took great pride in the fact that they had performed as well, if not better, than most volunteer soldiers in the Union Army, and had contributed significantly to the preservation of

[39] For a contemporary history of the 11th Indiana (three months), see David Stevenson, *Indiana's Roll of Honor* (Indianapolis: self published, 1864) 89–116. The service of the three years' regiment is detailed in Scribner, *Indiana's Roll of Honor*, 241–88.

the Union. Even many years after the war, the *Crawfordsville* (IN) *Daily Journal* believed that "this regiment stood apart, distinguished, admired and beloved, not only by those whose sons and brothers were in its ranks, but by the people of the State [of Indiana], both citizens and soldiers."[40] Perhaps Hoosier division commander and Vicksburg veteran General Alvin P. Hovey penned the best tribute to the men of the 11th Indiana. In his official report on the siege of that city, he succinctly explained to his superiors and to posterity why his hard-fighting Hoosiers and the other soldiers in his command had done so well: "They were veterans and determined to succeed."[41]

---

[40] *Crawfordsville Daily Journal,* 17 October 1889.
[41] *Official Records,* ser. 1, vol. 24, pt. 2, p. 241.

Chapter 1

JOINING UP

I will now give an outline of my life in the U.S. Volunteer Army during the war of the great Rebellion of 1861 to 1865, which is the real object of my writing these Memoirs. I was going to school to D. H. Heckathorn at old No. 5 school house when the first call for volunteers was made by President Lincoln,[5] in April 1861. For quite a while before this I had been keeping close watch on the signs of the times and had become fully convinced that there was going to be a war between the North and South. I had also determined if it came to a war that I would have a hand in it, as I lived about three miles from our little town of Waveland.[6] I had arranged with a friend by the name of Hatfield who lived in the town, that the moment he heard there was a call for volunteers he was to let me know. I had not hinted to my parents or anyone else except this friend that I had any thought of the army.

On the morning of April 17, 1861 I was up in my room trying to write my first essay—the teacher had ordered me to write one. My sisters had gone to school and had left the dinner bucket for me to bring. I was wrestling with my essay. I could think of nothing to write. I had worked myself up to a fever heat trying to dig up ideas

---

[5]William M. Heckathorn of Montgomery County, undoubtedly one of the schoolmaster's relatives, served as a private in Durham's Company G from 1861–1864 (William H. H. Terrell, *Report of the Adjutant General of the State of Indiana,* vol. 4 [Indianapolis: Samuel M. Douglass, 1866] 189).

[6] Waveland IN located in the southwestern part of Montgomery County, was laid out in 1835 and named for "a Kentucky gentleman's home." By the early 1880s the town had a population of about 800 (H. W. Beckwith, *History of Montgomery County* [Chicago: H. H. Hill and N. Iddings, 1881] 329–32).

and language to express them. My mind seemed blank, as if I had been sand-bagged. Just when I was in the last agonies of despair my friend Hatfield rushed in the room and told me there was a call for 75,000 volunteers for three months.[7] Without a word I changed my pen from my fingers to a firm grip in my hand and with much force drove the pen into the paper on which I was trying with such ill success to write my essay. Then springing from my chair and down into the room where my mother and a neighbor woman were enjoying a morning chat, I told my mother I would like to have a clean shirt. She wanted to know what I wanted with it and I told her I simply wanted a clean shirt. About this time she got sight of my friend and then her suspicions ran high and she knew that there was something "awful" going to happen. She continued to press the question as to why I wanted my shirt. I finally told her I was going away and she pressed the question harder as to where I was going. I finally told her I was going to "War." The idea of me going to war upset her completely. At first she positively forbade me going, then thinking I was of age she begged with many tears that I should not go. I told her my mind had been made up for quite a while to go and I was going. I had to find my shirt myself. I do not think she ever did forgive or like Hatfield afterward for informing me of the call. She never knew it was by my earnest request that he did so.

My father was down on the farm and I went to bid him goodbye. My mother followed me and was pleading with me not to go. When I informed my father of my intentions he said it would leave him in a pretty bad fix as I was his only dependence, but if I felt it was my duty to go it was all right and if it came to a pinch he said he would go too,

---

[7] In the call for volunteers after the firing on Fort Sumter, President Lincoln asked for six regiments (4,683 men) from Indiana. According to Indiana Adjutant General W. H. H. Terrell, more than 12,000 men volunteered in less than a week (Emma Lou Thornbrough, *Indiana in the Civil War Era, 1850–1880* [Indianapolis: Indiana Historical Bureau, 1965] 104, 124).

as he was yet a pretty good shot with a rifle. He told me he hoped I would bring back with me the scalp of my old namesake, Gov. Wise of Virginia.[8] My father had me get my saddle mule and ride to town. He went with me, but before we started my mother insisted on him buying a Bible for me as she could not bear the idea of me facing such dangers without a copy of the Holy Writ in my pocket.

My father could not find one to suit him in Waveland so he went with me to Crawfordsville, the county seat 16 miles from home, to purchase a bible for me.[9] He bought one and I carried it through the war and have it yet. The back is well worn and I am sorry to say it is not very badly "thumb-worn" on the inside. I had to go by the school house to deliver the dinner bucket to my sisters and when I informed them and the teacher where I was going, and bade them all goodbye, it is useless to say there was a tearful recess for a while.

When I got to Waveland I found four or five boys there, ready to go. It created quite a commotion in the little town when we left, as we were the first who had ever left the town for war. When we got to Crawfordsville my father gave me the bible, a twenty dollar gold piece and a father's advice and blessing. It had been my intention to join Captain Lew Wallace's Company, "The Montgomery Guards," but I found out it was filled to its full quota.[10]

---

[8] Durham was named for Henry Alexander Wise (1806–1876), a congressman from Virginia (1833–1844), minister to Brazil (1844–1847), and Democratic governor of Virginia (1856–1860). Once the Civil War began, Wise was commissioned a brigadier general in the Confederate Army and served until the end of the war (Patricia L. Faust, ed., *Historical Times Illustrated Encyclopedia of the Civil War* [New York: Harper Collins Publishers, 1986] 838–39; Barton H. Wise, *The Life of Henry A. Wise of Virginia, 1806–1876* [New York: The Macmillan Co., 1899]).

[9] Crawfordsville, the county seat of Montgomery County IN, contained more than 1,900 people in 1860. The county population was nearly 21,000 (Joseph C. G. Kennedy, *Population of the United States in 1860; Compiled from the Original Returns of the Eighth Census, under the Direction of the Secretary of the Interior* [Washington, DC:Government Printing Office, 1864] 112, 122).

[10] Lew Wallace had formed the Montgomery Guards, a local militia company, in 1856. The well-drilled unit modeled their dress on the uniform of the French North African Zouaves. When the Civil War began, sixty-two of the sixty-four members of the Guards enlisted in the Union Army (Lew Wallace, *An Autobiography*, vol. 1 [New York: Harper and Bros., 1906] 245–47).

I took the train that afternoon for Ladoga where I joined the "Ladoga Blues." I stayed that night at Ladoga where my sister Cora was going to boarding school.[11] Next day we went to Indianapolis. When I boarded the cars at Crawfordsville to go to Ladoga it was the first time I was ever in a railway car. I thought they ran "awful" fast and could not see why the train did not jump the track, but as a matter of fact the train was making less than 20 miles an hour.

When we got to Indianapolis we were met at the depot by a string band which furnished martial music for us to march by, to the State House. If one would judge the music by the step we kept, or rather did not keep, he would have thought it fearfully mixed music, for we were mostly all farmer boys and did not know any step except our good old swinging cornfield step. Every fellow had his own individual step. When we got to the State House we were marched into the basement where it was dark and gloomy with only a few dim gas jets burning. We were halted and "right-faced" with much difficulty and explanation, for none of us knew what "right-face," "left-face," or "front-face" meant. But we finally got all our faces in one direction and found Lew Wallace, who was then Adjutant General of the State, in front of us.

Wallace, who had a powerful voice, administered the oath to us with great solemnity, swearing us into the State service.[12] Then he addressed us, saying: "Now boys, you are no longer citizens, but

---

[11] Ladoga was a substantial community before the Civil War, containing, among other businesses, four physicians, a number of dry goods and grocery dealers, several blacksmiths, a flouring and grist mill, and a woolen factory (*Ladoga* [IN] *Ruralist*, 27 April 1860). Durham's sister Ruth Cordelia was born 25 April 1844, the seventh of nine Durham children.

[12] Wallace's term as state adjutant general was short lived. He was appointed 14 April 1861 and officially commissioned the following day. On 26 April he was commissioned colonel of the 11th Indiana. Durham and his comrades were first sworn into state service, then later into federal service (Wallace, *An Autobiography*, vol. 1, 261–69; Terrell, *Report of the Adjutant General*, [Indianapolis: W. R. Holloway, 1865] vol. 2, x, 27). The full text of the oath of allegiance taken by volunteers to the State of Indiana may be found in Alan D. Gaff, *On Many A Bloody Field: Four Years in the Iron Brigade* (Bloomington: Indiana University Press, 1996) 11.

soldiers. It is your duty to obey orders. This war will not be over in
three months or a year, but will be a long and bloody conflict. Some
of you will get home and some of you will not." His great voice rolled
up through the rotunda, echoing and re-echoing, and with the
gloomy surroundings and the wonderful force of Wallace's words and
voice, I think I was worse scared then than [sic] I ever was in battle. I
was greatly impressed with the idea that someone was going to get
hurt, and perhaps badly hurt, before the conflict was over. I felt very
shaky. We were then marched to the old Bates House for supper.

It was the largest hotel in the city and very few of us had ever
been in a hotel before. They had young ladies as waiters and of course
we were all embarrassed and made many bad breaks in table
etiquette. One fellow, sitting next to me, when the girl asked him if he
wished his steak "rare" or "done," thought he would find out by
ordering his steak rare as he did not know what "rare" or "done"
meant. When it was brought to him with the blood oozing out of it,
he looked at it for quite a while and then turning to the girl he told
her in a very subdued manner that he wished she would take that
steak back and have it "rared" over again.

We then went to the old army barracks for a few days and then
we camped on the fair grounds where we began to drill right.[13] All of
the companies, which were known as the State Guards, volunteered.
They were the only military organizations Indiana had before the
war. They were well drilled. Captain Lew Wallace's Montgomery
Guards was the crack drill company of the State. These companies

[13] Durham is probably mistaken here. It appears that the 11th Indiana was quartered first at Camp Morton (the Indiana State Fairgrounds), but when the area became crowded Wallace had his men moved to the "old Bellefontaine car shop." Wallace states in his memoirs that he had an old freight depot converted into a barracks, and marched his men from Camp Morton to that location (Hattie Lou Winslow and Joseph R. H. Moore, *Camp Morton, 1861–1865: Indianapolis Prison Camp* [Indianapolis: Indiana Historical Society, 1940] 242; Wallace, *An Autobiography*, vol. 1, 268–69). It is possible that Durham thought the building was in fact an old army barracks, and merely recalled the events in reverse order.

were filled to the regulation one hundred men with the new volunteers who wished to get into the different companies. Lew Wallace formed these companies into a Regiment which was numbered the Eleventh Indiana Volunteer Regiment. As Wallace adopted the Zouave drill, the regiment was known in the state and the army as "The Eleventh Indiana Zouaves."[14] Lew Wallace then resigned his position as Adjutant General of the state and was commissioned Colonel of this regiment.

The women of Indianapolis made a flag and banner for the regiment and when the time came for them to present these colors to the regiment, Colonel Wallace marched us to the State House grounds, formed us in a solid column and accepted the colors from the ladies.[15] He made a speech in which he explained how it was that the Second Indiana Regiment, of which he, Wallace, was a Lieutenant, was disgraced by order of Jeff Davis, who was then in command of the American troops at the Battle of Buena Vista, Mexico, during the war with Mexico. He said Col. Booles [sic], the Colonel of the 2d Indiana Regiment was a coward and ordered the regiment to retreat when there was no occasion for a retreat. This caused General Jeff Davis to issue the order, disgracing the Indiana troops, and I will just state here that Col. Booles was the leader of the "Knights of the Golden Circle" in Indiana during the war of the Rebellion, an organi-

---

[14] For a description of the 11th's Zouave drill, see Wallace, *An Autobiography*, vol. 1, 270, 273–74.

[15] The ladies of Terre Haute made a beautiful silk US flag for the regiment, while the ladies of Indianapolis gave the unit a "rich blue flag, fringed with gold, and bearing the National coat of arms." Both flags were inscribed "Indiana Zouaves—11th Regiment." The ceremony was described as "a most impressive scene and filled hundreds of manly eyes with tears," a "grand gala day" when all Indianapolis and the surrounding country turned out to witness the presentation (*Indianapolis Daily Journal*, 9 May 1861).

[16] Durham is somewhat confused in his recollections. Lew Wallace was a lieutenant in the 1st Indiana Infantry Regiment during the Mexican War, and was not involved in the Battle of Buena Vista (Wallace, *An Autobiography*, vol. 1, 114–15). William A. Bowles (c.1799–1873), a physician in Orange County IN, was elected colonel of the Second Indiana Infantry. At the Battle of Buena Vista (23 February 1847), while facing an overwhelming Mexican assault, Bowles became confused and ordered his regiment to

zation in the North who opposed the Union and sympathized with the Southern rebels.[16] They tried to keep men from volunteering, resisted drafts, tried to get Union soldiers to desert, tried to release our prisoners we had sent North and did everything in their power to obstruct the success of the Union army. We called them "copper heads" after the most treacherous and poisonous viper in the world. They were well named for they were too cowardly to go to their friends in the South and fight for their cause but would assassinate in the dark. They were most heartily despised by all Union men and were looked on with contempt by the rebels, for the South had no use for a friend or sympathizer who was too cowardly to go to the field of battle and help them fight for their cause.

After Col. Wallace explained the cause of the disgrace to the Indiana soldiers at Buena Vista, he told us that now we were going to fight the man, Jeff Davis, President of the so-called Southern Confederacy, the man who disgraced them by his order.[17] He said we had a two-fold purpose to perform, we not only had our duty as

---

retreat. His troops fell back in disorder, then rallied and fought bravely during the remainder of the battle, but accusations of cowardice haunted Bowles, his men, and the entire state well into the Civil War period. During the latter conflict Bowles adopted a pro-Southern stance, was accused of membership in the "Knights of the Golden Circle," an organization opposed to the Lincoln administration, and was finally tried for treason in Indianapolis in 1864. Although sentenced to death, Bowles was eventually released (G. R. Tredway, *Democratic Opposition to the Lincoln Administration in Indiana* [Indianapolis: Indiana Historical Bureau, 1973] 136–44, 224–55).

[17] Jefferson Davis commanded the 1st Mississippi Regiment at Buena Vista, and his timely arrival after the retreat of the Second Indiana helped halt the Mexican advance and save the day for the Americans. In his official report of the battle dated 2 March 1847, Davis failed to mention that the majority of the members of the 2nd Indiana subsequently reformed and returned to the fight. He merely reported that Colonel Bowles and a small group of Indiana troops attached themselves to his command and fought alongside the Mississippians. This fact, combined with American commander General Zachary Taylor's praise for his former son-in-law and his Mississippi Regiment, contributed to Davis's unpopularity with the Hoosier veterans of Buena Vista. Some Hoosiers even argued that Davis influenced General Taylor to slight the 2nd Indiana in his official report (James T. McIntosh, ed., *The Papers of Jefferson Davis*, vol. 3 [Baton Rouge: Louisiana State University Press, 1981] 139–49, 166–67; Oran Perry, *Indiana in the Mexican War* [Indianapolis: Adjutant General's Office, 1908] 303–304). In 1861, with the inauguration of Davis as president of the Confederacy, this resentment intensified until it became easy for Indiana residents to believe that Davis had in fact originated the whole Buena Vista "slander."

soldiers to perform but we had, by our bravery, to wipe out the stain that Jeff Davis had placed upon Indiana soldiers at Buena Vista. He then said: "Now boys, down on your knees, raise your right hands to high heaven and take a solemn oath to remember Buena Vista." It was a dramatic sight to see the whole regiment drop to their knees, with up-lifted hands, swearing to remember Buena Vista. This did more to entuse [sic] the patriotic spirit of Indiana than all else that had happened. All leading papers of the country had pictures of Wallace's Zouaves on their knees taking the oath to remember Buena Vista—in fact it electrified the whole North.[18]

We wore the Zouave uniform, which was gray, the coat or jacket cut rounding in front and had no buttons; it was fastened in front with a loop and was just long enough to reach to the waist band of the pants. The jacket was bound with red cord and red braid on each breast. We wore knee pants with leggings and the knee band and waist band were tight but the body of the pants was extremely baggy. The cap was gray with a red crown. After the first three month's service, we discarded the gray uniform and only retained the Zouave jacket which was made of regulation blue with red cord all around the front and bottom or lower edge of the jacket. We also had a flower of red braid on each breast. After the first three month's service, the commissioned officers wore the regulation dress uniform of blue.[19]

---

[18] Wallace, *An Autobiography*, vol. 1, 270–72. For an illustration of the ceremony in the popular press, see *Harper's Weekly*, 22 June 1861.

[19] Wallace agrees with this description of the first (three months) uniform in his *Autobiography*, vol. 1, 270. Also see Don Troiani, Earl J. Coates, and James L. Kochan, *Don Troiani's Soldiers in America, 1754–1865* (Mechanicsburg PA: Stackpole Books, 1998) 159–60. A color plate and description of the later uniform of the 11th Indiana (a blue jacket with blue trim, not red, as Durham remembered) may be found in John R. Elting and Michael J. McAfee, eds., *Long Endure: The Civil War Period, 1852–1867* (Novato CA: Presidio Press, 1982) 44–45. For a photograph of one of the unit's members see Michael J. McAfee, "Uniforms and History: 11th Regiment Indiana Zouaves, 1861," in *Military Images* 17/6 (May–June 1996): 35–36.

I think it was the next day after we received our colors that we left Indianapolis and went to Evansville, Indiana, on the Ohio River, for the purpose of stopping boats from carrying contraband goods down the river to the enemy.[20] Our regiment was the first to leave Indianapolis at the breaking out of the war. We had a battery of cannon on the bank of the river from which we would fire a shot in front of every boat that tried to get down the river without stopping to be examined. If they refused to heave-to, the next shot would be at the boat.

While camped on the river near Evansville, I was taken with something like the cholera and was doubled up like a jack-knife with cramps. I thought my time had about come when some of the boys found me and carried me to the surgeon's tent. The surgeon, Dr. Thomas Fry, who had known me from my infancy and who pretended to be a great friend of my father, gave me a dose of opiates and left me lying on the ground.[21] This was about noon and the opiates put me to sleep at once. I did not wake up until nearly noon the next day and found myself still lying on the ground where he had doped me. I never had any use for him after that for I knew he could have given me better treatment if he had wished to. I do not think that I have ever seen a man who was so puffed up with vanity on account of a little position as was Dr. Fry and I have seen some wonderfully puffed men. He became bigoted and offensive to sensible men.

---

[20] Durham is correct. The flag presentation took place on 8 May, and the regiment left for Evansville the following evening (9 May).

[21] Thomas W. Fry Sr. of Crawfordsville was commissioned surgeon of the 11th Indiana (three months) on 26 April 1861. He served until the regiment was mustered out, then was surgeon for the 11th Indiana (three years) until appointed brigade surgeon in September 1861 (Terrell, *Report of the Adjutant General,* vol. 2, 27, 76). Fry was brevetted a lieutenant colonel of volunteers in October 1865 for faithful and meritorious service, and was mustered out of the army the following month. He died on 24 February 1873 (Francis B. Heitman, *Historical Register and Dictionary of the United States Army,* vol. 1 [Washington, DC: Government Printing Office, 1903] 439).

The next day, after I awoke from the effects of the dope the doctor had given me, we left Evansville for Cumberland, Maryland. I was still sick and unable to sit up. It was the 6th day of June we left Evansville. We got to Greensburg, Indiana at noon. The citizens of the town had a royal dinner prepared for us and young ladies brought the food into the cars and distributed it to the soldiers. As I was still sick and unable to sit up they gave me many kind words and shed sympathetic tears (I was the first sick soldier the girls had ever seen). They threw the "hardtack" out of my haversack and filled it with good things so if I should get well before it became stale, I would have a feast.[22] I did not get well in time to enjoy the food, but I wish to say 'God bless the girls and the good people of Greensburg.'

---

[22] Hardtack was the army bread ration, consisting of large, hard crackers. The bland taste of hardtack was often made worse by the presence of worms or mould (John D. Billings, *Hardtack and Coffee: The Unwritten Story of Army Life* [Boston: George M. Smith & Co., 1888; reprint, Chicago: R. R. Donnelley & Sons Co., 1960] 113–19).

Chapter 2

WESTERN VIRGINIA

When we arrived at Cumberland, Md., we went into camp on the same ground that General George Washington camped on at the breaking out of the Revolutionary War, and we got water at the same spring that his troops did. There was part of an old flag pole on the camp ground that the citizens claimed was the flag pole Washington raised while camped there, but I had my doubts about it, notwithstanding the evidence of its having stood there for many years.[23]

I was still sick when I got to Cumberland and unable to march to camp from the railroad. My captain (Montgomery Carr) told me to get into the baggage car and lie there until wagons were sent for the baggage and to ride to camp in one of the wagons.[24] All the cars

---

[23] The 11th Indiana occupied Cumberland on 10 June (US War Department, *The War of the Rebellion: A Compilation of the Official Records of the Union and Confederate Armies* [Washington, DC: Government Printing Office, 1880–1901] ser. 1, vol. 2, p. 105). The site Durham refers to is probably Fort Cumberland, built by colonial forces in late 1754 during the French and Indian War. Washington traveled to the area several times during that war as a Virginia militia officer. He last appeared at the old fort in October 1794, when he reviewed troops assembled to take part in the Whiskey Rebellion. The fort rapidly disappeared following its abandonment, so Durham is probably correct that little if any of the post remained when the Hoosiers arrived (Work Projects Administration, *Maryland: A Guide to the Old Line State* [New York: Oxford University Press, 1940] 264–67; James Thomas Flexner, *George Washington: The Forge of Experience, 1732–1775* [Boston: Little, Brown & Co., 1965] 122–23, 138, 196–98, and *George Washington: Anguish and Farewell, 1793–1799* [Boston: Little, Brown & Co., 1969] 176).

[24] Henry M. Carr of Crawfordsville IN was commissioned captain of Company G, 11th Indiana (three months) on 22 April 1861. He served until the regiment was mustered out and then reentered the army as captain of Company G in the 11th Indiana, three years' service. His service with the company was short-lived, however, as he was promoted to colonel of the 58th Indiana in November 1861 (William H. H. Terrell, *Report of the Adjutant General of the State of Indiana*, vol. 2 [Indianapolis: Samuel M. Douglass, 1866] 30, 81).

except the baggage car had been taken away. When I went to get in the car, Frank Gill of my company who was guarding the baggage, refused to let me in and swore he would bayonet me if I did not get clear away from the car.[25] He knew I was sick and barely able to stand on my feet. I told him the Captain had ordered me to lie in the car until the wagons came for the baggage, but it was no go, he would not even let me lie in the shade of the car, so I had to lie for hours in the broiling sun. If I had had a cartridge for my gun I think my first shot in that great war would have been at him. I would have licked him after I got well but did not feel that would be adequate punishment. I sought an excuse to give him the full punishment he deserved but I did not get the opportunity as he left the service at the expiration of our three month's service. I have never seen the villian [sic] since and I hope I never will for as I grow older my vengeance grows greater at his cussedness.

On our arrival at Cumberland, Col. Wallace detailed thirteen men of the regiment for scouts and had I not been sick at the time I would have been one of the scouts. These scouts were placed under command of Corporal Hay, who was a soldier in the Mexican War and was a fighter and a daredevil from away back.[26] It was the duty of these scouts, who were well mounted, to scout the country over for miles around our camp and report if the enemy was found approaching. On the 26th of June, while our scouts were going up the Potomac River on the Virginia side, they met a squad of Col. Mosby's

---

[25] Private Franklin Gill of Montgomery County was mustered into Company G, 11th Indiana on 22 April 1861 and served until mustered out on 4 August 1861 (Terrell, *Report of the Adjutant General*, vol. 4, 69). Gill survived the war and died on 20 June 1915, in Oakwood, Vermilion County IL, after suffering from measles, chronic diarrhea, and the resulting diseases of the stomach, liver, and rectum, contracted after the regiment's return from Romney VA (Franklin Gill pension record, RG 15, National Archives and Records Administration, Washington, DC).

[26] Corporal David B. Hay of Company A, 11th Indiana, hailed from Marion County IN. He was mustered into service on 22 April 1861 and served until mustered out on 4 August (Wallace, *An Autobiography*, vol. 1 [New York: Harper and Bros., 1906] 297–98; Terrell, *Report of the Adjutant General*, vol. 4, 62).

(afterward General Mosby) Virginia Black Horse Cavalry. Our scouts made a dash at them, overtook them and had a running saber fight. Our scouts killed several of the rebel squad and Corporal Hay received several severe saber cuts on his head and face. They soon ran onto a whole company of the Black Horse Cavalry under command of Captain Ashby.[27]

Our scouts then retreated to an island in the Potomac River, known as Kelley's Island. They made their stand on this island where they had a great advantage over the enemy as the enemy had to ford the river to get to them. Our scouts picked many of the enemy off their horses while trying to ford the river to the island. Some of them succeeded in getting onto the island and a desperate hand-to-hand fight ensued. Captain Ashby got McFarland, one of the scouts down and was in the act of plunging a large bowie knife in him when James R. Hallowell, one of the scouts, took his gun by the barrel and dealt Captain Ashby a fearful blow on the head. He drove the hammer of his gun into the Captain's head. The blow broke the stock off the gun and killed Captain Ashby instantly. As Hallowell's gun was now disabled, he took a brace of fine large Navy revolvers off of Captain Ashby's body and used them during the remainder of the battle. Later in the war Hallowell was Colonel of the 31st Indiana Infantry and after the war, a brother-in-law of mine.

Our scouts killed thirty-one of the rebels in this fight. Only one of the scouts (Hollenbeck) was badly wounded. When night came on our scouts escaped from the island, leaving Hollenbeck on the island, as they knew the rebels would be reinforced. As soon as our scouts

---

[27] Actually John S. Mosby was a member of the 1st Virginia ("Black Horse") Cavalry, but Captain Richard Ashby, brother of legendary Confederate cavalry General Turner Ashby, commanded Company A, 7th Virginia Cavalry. Mortally wounded in the skirmish with Wallace's scouts, Ashby died about 3 July and is buried with his brother in Winchester VA (Channing M. Smith, "General Turner Ashby," *Confederate Veteran*, vol. 32 [July 1924]: 286; R. A. Brock, ed., *Southern Historical Society Papers*, vol. 29 [Richmond VA: By the Society, 1901] 137, and vol. 35, 335).

got back to the regiment we immediately started to the scene of the battle but when we reached the island we found the enemy had left, taking Hollenbeck with them. We pursued them until we came to a farm house where they had halted and there we found Hollenbeck on the porch, dead.[28] We learned that the enemy had received information here of our pursuit and had bayonetted Hollebeck to death and lit out. We followed them no farther. We brought Hollenbeck's body back to camp and buried him with "Honors of War," which was the first funeral of the kind I had ever seen—much less participated in. The whole regiment followed the corpse to the grave with reverse arms. It was very impressive.[29]

In the latter part of June (I have forgotten the exact date) we marched to Romney, Va., where we had learned there was a body of the enemy camped. We surprised them and had quite a lively little battle. We soon routed them, killing and wounding a number and took several prisoners, among whom was the Colonel of a rebel regiment. I have forgotten his name. We lost none and but few were wounded. This was our regiment's first battle. We thought it a very large affair at the time but found out later on that it was not so large as it appeared to us then.[30]

We celebrated the Fourth of July at camp by making all the commissioned officers of the regiment stand guard over the camp. We put Col. Wallace in as Corporal of the guard.[31] We gave them very

---

[28] John C. Hollenbeck of Marion County IN enlisted in Company B of the 11th Indiana on 22 April 1861. He was killed on 27 June (Terrell, *Report of the Adjutant General*, vol. 4, 64).

[29] Detailed accounts of this action may be found in Wallace, *An Autobiography*, vol. 1, 297–307; in *Official Records*, ser. 1, vol. 2, pp. 134–35; and in the *Indianapolis Daily Journal*, 4 July 1861. Kelley's Island is located where Patterson's Creek meets the Potomac River, about ten miles southeast of Cumberland .

[30] The skirmish at Romney VA took place on 13 June 1861, rather than the latter part of June, as Durham remembered. The Confederate officer taken prisoner was Major Isaac Vandever (*Official Records*, ser. 1, vol. 2, 123–24).

[31] Durham is correct in his description. The camp was cleaned and decorated, swings were built, and one company performed gymnastic exercises. Along with enjoying a feast served by the citizens of Cumberland, and visits by local ladies, enlisted men assumed the posts of colonel, lieutenant colonel,

strict orders not to let anything cross their beat and if anyone tried to cross the line they were to order halt three times and then shoot if they failed to halt. About the only casualty was when a hog tried to cross Lieutenant John Ramsey's beat.[32] He "halted" it three times according to orders and as the hog persisted in crossing the line, he shot and killed it. As the hog belonged to a loyal citizen, we chipped in and paid him for the hog.

We received word one night that the enemy had crossed the Potomac and intended to attack Cumberland that night. We were marched out through the town about 2 o'clock in the morning, to take a position for the defense of the town. I was greatly impressed with one thing as we marched through the main street of the city. About three hundred of the loyal citizens, both male and female, had gathered on a large balcony and as the regiment marched in the street beneath them, they sang "The Star Spangled Banner." The stillness of the night and the solemnity of the occasion of us marching out to meet the enemy made it very impressive. I thought the song at that time very appropriate.

After we took our position and formed our line of defense, I was sent out on picket duty. I was stationed by a cedar bush with orders not to move until I saw the enemy coming and then fire on the enemy and fall back to the line of defense. In all my experience I do not think I ever had such a hard time to keep awake as I did that

---

major, and adjutant. The officers were kept on guard duty for three and a half hours before being relieved. A lieutenant in the regiment wrote "It was a laughable scene to see our staff, our surgeons, our captains and lieutenants walking the rounds on the sentinel's beat." Two or three hogs were shot for entering the camp after being ordered to halt, the quartermaster was put on extra duty for sitting down at his post, and Dr. Fry was reprimanded for shooting at a mountain because it would not advance and give the countersign. The Zouaves made the day a festival, with dancing, jumping, swinging, national songs, and band music, and forgot "all danger, hardships, and inconveniences" (*Indianapolis Daily Journal*, 10 July 1861; *Crawfordsville* (IN) *Weekly Review*, 13 July 1861).

[32] John W. Ramsey of Indianapolis was a second lieutenant in Company K of the 11th Indiana. He was commissioned in April 1861 (Terrell, *Report of the Adjutant General*, [Indianapolis: W. R. Holloway, 1865] vol. 2, 31).

night on picket duty. The penalty for being found asleep on picket duty is death. Had I been allowed to move around some it would not have been so hard to keep awake, but to maintain perfectly still I suffered fearfully. I managed to keep my eyes open but could not have seen a regiment of the enemy ten feet away. But the enemy did not come—it proved to be a false alarm of which we had many during the war.

About the 6th or 7th of July we started on the march to Martinsburg, Va. The first day or two Col. Wallace had me guard the Colonel-prisoner we had captured at Romney, but when Wallace found I was about the only one in the regiment who had any money, he put me in charge of the sick in the ambulances so I could buy such food from those living along the line of march as the sick could eat. While crossing Fairview mountain in Maryland, we encountered the heaviest rain I had ever seen or ever expect to see. We were on top of the mountain and the rainfall was so great one could not see a person ten feet away. The water was half-knee deep on the ground and we were right in the cloud. After this cloud had passed over the mountain I found myself for the first time above the clouds, the whole Potomac valley below me was covered by a black angry cloud. It was a grand sight to stand above the clouds and look down on them and see the flashes of lightning and hear the peals of thunder below us. This mountain is called "Fairview Mountain" from the fact that when a person is on top of the mountain he can see three states, viz: Pennsylvania, Virginia and Maryland. It is a grand view.

That night after being so drenched with the rain, we bivouacked at a little village near the foot of the mountain, called Clear Springs. I got the sick boys comfortably located in an old cotton gin and the regiment bivouacked a little distance from the town. After I got the sick cared for I concluded to take a look at the town before going to camp. While walking down the main street, I saw a young lady standing at the gate in front of a nice looking house. Before I got opposite to her I saw she was a very intelligent looking girl. To my surprise in passing the gate she spoke to me and asked if I would not like to have some supper. As a soldier is always as ready to eat as a ⸫ hobo, I expressed my willingness—notwithstanding we were very doubtful as to what people that far south would dish up to a Union soldier. But I thought her too nice looking to be a "poisoning Reb." I was still as wet from that "mountain dew" we passed through on Fairview Mountain as if I had just been baptized into the Campbellite Church and had been given a second dip to make sure my sins were washed away.

The beautiful damsel took me in the house and gave me a drink of very fine brandy, built a fire to dry my clothes by, and I wondered at her kindness for I knew I was not half as beautiful as she. But I soon found she was a loyal Union girl and she was doing all this for the cause. That relieved my mind as it was a mystery to me why I should be so attractive to such a beautiful girl. I had a royal supper and she had baked a cherry pie for me. If there was anything I liked better than another, it was more cherry pie. After supper I did not feel in any hurry to get out to camp and she insisted on me staying all night with them, and as an inducement she said she would have her school chum come over and they would entertain me with music.[33] As my soul was always hungry for music I could not resist, even at the penalty of being court-martialed and shot. In the meantime I had learned her father was Mayor of the town and a staunch Union man and this daughter and her girl chum had just returned from college

---

[33] Durham was not the only one in the regiment who was well treated by the citizens of Clear Spring. S. S. Goldsberry of the regiment wrote that the "very hospitable citizens" quartered the men in local churches and did all they could to make the Hoosiers comfortable. Goldsberry himself ate dinner at the home of a married woman, dried his clothes, and was furnished with dry socks, slippers, and lemonade (*Indianapolis Daily Journal*, 19 July 1861).

where they had graduated. The girl chum came over and they were both fine performers on the piano and good vocalists. They entertained me until midnight and then the girl lighted me to bed—a nice clean feather bed—which was the only bed I slept in during the war, except when home on leave of absence. The next morning when I came down to breakfast she gave me a nice eye opener of brandy and after breakfast, when taking my reluctant departure, she handed me my haversack. All the hardtack and sowbelly had been thrown out and the sack washed and filled with viands (and cherry pie).[34] I remember that as the most pleasant night I spent during the war. I was so certain that I would never forget the girl's name that I did not take the precaution to write her name in my diary. I fully intended to write her as I had promised to do but before I found courage to write to her the excitement of war had caused her name to pass from my memory forever. All I can do now is cherish a fond memory of her and say "God bless her."

After our night's bivouac at Clear Springs, Md., we continued our march to Williamsport where we waded the Potomac River. The water was armpit deep. As soon as we got across to the Virginia side of the river we arrived where there had been a lively skirmish a week or more before. The rebels had been defeated by our troops and in their haste to get away they had buried their dead so shallow we could see their hands and feet sticking out of the ground and hogs were eating the carcasses. This was the first human putrification that I had ever smelled and the Lord knows I never wanted to smell it again— but I did. I think it was the worst stench I ever met up with.

We reached Martinsburg, Virginia, that night, which was July 11th. We were halted on a street in front of a house where I saw a

---

34 "Sowbelly" was soldier slang for salt pork, part of the army meat ration (John D. Billings, *Hardtack and Coffee: The Unwritten Story of Army Life* [Boston: George M. Smith & Co., 1887; reprint, Chicago: R. R. Donnelley & Sons Co., 1960] 135).

light burning and there appeared to be some kind of a commotion in the house. I went in to see what was going on and I found a girl of about 20 years of age who had been frightened to death the night before. A deserter from the rebel army had gone to the house the night before and raised the window where the girl and her grandmother were sleeping. The old lady was sleeping next to the window and the girl by her side. The fellow commenced stabbing the old lady with a knife. The girl woke up, saw the fellow stabbing her grandmother and it frightened her to death. This was the first case of the kind I had ever seen. She was a horrible sight with the fearful fright so plainly stamped on her face. It was a sight I never can forget. The man was caught, court-martialed and shot according to military law. The military way of executing the death penalty is to detail thirteen soldiers with empty guns. The officer in charge of the squad loads the guns and twelve of the guns are loaded with ball and one is loaded with a blank cartridge. He hands these guns to the squad and none of them know which gun contains the blank cartridge, therefore cannot tell who fired it. The man to be executed is tied to a tree and the squad is halted ten paces in front of him. The officer in command of the squad gives the order "Ready, aim, fire," and they all fire at once and the villain is done for.

At Martinsburg we were placed in command of General Patterson.[35] He commanded that post and had about 30,000 soldiers

---

[35] Major General Robert Patterson assumed command of the Department of Pennsylvania in late April 1861. He occupied Harper's Ferry and Martinsburg (West) VA, that summer, but accomplished little else and was soon discharged from the army. Durham overestimates the size of Patterson's army, but does correctly note that Patterson was supposed to keep Confederate General Joseph E. Johnston's forces from leaving the Shenandoah Valley to help oppose a Union drive from Washington, DC, to Manassas Junction VA. Patterson failed to keep Johnston in place, and his Confederates greatly contributed to the disastrous Union defeat at the Battle of First Bull Run on 21 July 1861 (Frank J. Welcher, *The Union Army, 1861–1865*, vol. 1 [Bloomington: Indiana University Press, 1989] 73). Patterson's lengthy defense of his actions may be found in his book, *A Narrative of the Campaign in the Valley of the Shenandoah in 1861*, published in 1865 by John Campbell of Philadelphia.

in his command. The rebel, General Joseph E. Johnson [sic], was stationed at Winchester, Virginia, a few miles from Martinsburg. General Patterson was ordered to engage Johnson and keep him from reinforcing the enemy at Bull Run where the first real battle of the war was to be fought. Patterson was a rebel sympathizer and had a son who was a Colonel in the rebel army.[36] He would not engage Johnson as he was ordered to do, but instead he moved us to Charlestown, ten miles from Harpers Ferry. We could hear the battle raging at Bull Run and could hear the trains carrying Johnson's army to the battle field.[37] Subordinate officers begged Patterson to let them intercept Johnson but he would not and the result was that Johnson reinforced the enemy at Bull Run and our army was disasterously defeated and driven pellmell back to Washington. However, this defeat was the best thing that could have happened to our army as they were over-confident. It taught them that they had something to do and they resolved to do it. We found we had a foe worthy of our steel and would take desperate fighting to conquer them. Many of our soldiers, when they enlisted in the first three month's service, thought it a kind of picnic outing but the battle of Bull Run demonstrated the fact to them that it was a real war with all its horrors. They began to realize that war was what General Sherman found it to be when he said "War is Hell." General Patterson was relieved of his

[36] Durham probably refers to General Patterson's son Colonel William Houston Patterson, born in Philadelphia, who died in Russellville TN in September 1904. His military service in the Confederate Army is unknown (S. A. Cunningham, "Col. William Houston Patterson," *Confederate Veteran*, vol. 13 [May 1905]: 236).

[37] Durham no doubt recalls these events incorrectly. Lew Wallace agrees that his men heard the trains in motion carrying General Joseph Johnston's troops toward Manassas, but not only was Durham hearing battle noises before the Battle of First Bull Run occurred, it is impossible that even on the day of the battle the sound could carry all the way to Winchester (Wallace, *An Autobiography*, vol. 1, 319–20).

[38] In the words of one 11th Indiana historian, when word of the Bull Run disaster arrived in camp, "the open and defiant denunciation of General Patterson as he rode through the camps of his army...was of such character as to preclude any description" (Henry C. Adams Jr., *Indiana at Vicksburg* [Indianapolis: Wm. B. Burford, 1911] 212). The citizens of Dayton, Ohio, noticed that the Hoosiers "complain bitterly, and declare that two regiments of their men could so have obstructed the progress" of Johnston that he would have been unable to join the fighting at First Bull Run (*Indianapolis Daily Journal*, 30 July 1861).

command for neglect of duty.[38] In the early part of the war we had trouble because of the treachery of some of our officers of high rank, and of cowardice of others, but the most of them were taken out of the service in the early days of the war.

We arrived at Charlestown, Virginia, July 17th. This was a strong rebel town and it was here that Old Osowatoma John Brown was hung and where he was confined in jail from the time of his capture until his execution. I saw the scaffold that he was hung on and it was made of walnut timber. I also saw the bullet holes where the Virginia Guards, in order to show their bravery and their animosity toward Brown, had shot the scaffold and Brown's body while he was being executed.[39] I went into the jail in which John Brown had been confined and saw the table on which he wrote his farewell letter to his wife. Near Harpers Ferry I saw the old log school house in which old John Brown had his guns and ammunition stored. With the old bowie knife I gave to John W. Durham I chipped off a piece of the scaffold, the table and the old school house to keep as trophies. I left them at home when I returned from the three month's service but after the war I found they had been misplaced and I never could find them. They would be greatly appreciated as relics now while "John Brown's soul is still marching on."[40]

As history gives an account of John Brown's escape into Virginia to inaugurate an uprising of the negroes I will not bother my readers with a recount. I will simply say that Brown was a strong abolitionist. He thought slavery a curse and he fought the "Border Ruffians" in

---

[39] "Old Osawatomie" John Brown (1800–1859), so named because of his May 1856 massacre of pro-slavery civilians near Osawatomie KS seized the US Arsenal at Harper's Ferry VA in October 1859. Brown was captured, tried, and hanged in Charlestown VA on 2 December 1859, without the help of militia gunfire. Durham was no doubt repeating local lore or else making a supposition about the bullet holes.

[40] Durham was not the only Hoosier to bring back relics of his service. Other men in the 11th Indiana returned with cannon balls, flags, remnants of the Harper's Ferry armory, caps, sashes, and "every sort of transportable military relics" from their time in the East (*Indianapolis Daily Journal*, 30 July 1861).

Kansas who were trying to make Kansas a slave state. He, with four or five others, then went to Harpers Ferry, Virginia, for the purpose of getting the negroes of the south to rebel against their slavery. I have always thought that his object in selecting Harpers Ferry as his base of operations was on account of the large gun factory there. I think it was his intention, when the proper time came, to seize the factory and arm his negroes with the guns in the factory. He and his party were captured, condemned to death and were executed by order of Governor Henry A. Wise, the man for whom I was named. When I started to the army my father requested me to bring back with me the scalp of my old namesake, Wise, but I was too busy to call on the gentleman and had to be content with bringing back a small piece of the scalp of his cause.

At Charlestown we camped on the plantation of old Col. Davenport, near the town. I saw a daughter of Henry Clay at Davenport's house, she having been married to a son of the old Colonel.[41] Her husband was at that time a Colonel in the rebel army.

On July 21st we left Charlestown and marched to Harpers Ferry, a distance of ten miles. In marching through Charlestown our regiment was thrown into platoons. When we were counted off I was number 1 of the second platoon. To my left was a guy fresh from college who had been kicking my heels in our drill until they were very sore. I knew he did it on purpose, presuming I was a country Jake that he could run over. I had cautioned him several times about it and as I saw it was pure cussedness in him I was getting pretty hot. When we were wheeling into platoons he gave me a vicious shove and told me I belonged to the left of the first platoon. It angered me and when I was bringing my gun down to fire at him, Lieutenant Dave

---

[41] Durham is mistaken. Henry Clay had a total of six daughters, but none lived until 1861 (Robert V. Remini, *Henry Clay: Statesman for the Union* [New York: W. W. Norton & Co, 1991] frontispiece).

Knox caught my gun and thereby saved a very poor soldier. After the war the fellow apologized to me and said I was aiming to serve him as he deserved and expressed himself as being pleased with the lesson it taught him.

In marching through the main street of Charlestown there was a rather amusing incident. Our platoons covered the full width of the street and a sergeant was walking on the sidewalk. A rebel girl who thought to show her great interest in the cause was standing in a door by the sidewalk. When our sergeant got opposite her she spat in his face. Quick as a flash he threw his arm around her neck, drew her to his breast and holding her as tight as if she were in a vice, he kissed her about a dozen times while the whole regiment was cheering. It was far greater punishment than it would have been had he knocked her senseless. I am betting a coon skin she never spit in another Yankee's face.

Harpers Ferry is a very picturesque place. It is located on the point between the Potomac and Shenandoah rivers where the Shenandoah empties into the Potomac and there are high mountains all around the town. The town is in the narrow valley and on the north side is a high, perpendicular bluff. About 25 or 30 feet from this bluff is a rock in the shape of a pyramid with a flat rock on the apex, making it look like a large table with a center post beneath it. It is known as the "Table Rock." It was on this rock that Cook (one of old John Brown's men) was married. He placed a long plank from the bluff to the table rock and he and his intended crossed onto it while the preacher stood in the valley below and performed the ceremony.[42] About all the enterprise of this little town was the arsenal and gun factory, which the rebels destroyed by fire before our troops got possession of the town.

On July 24th we started for home as our three month's service had expired. We marched through Sheperdstown [sic] to

Hagerstown, Maryland. We marched 26 miles in a half day as we were headed for home and each fellow tried his speed and durability. I was among the first to reach Hagerstown. Men of the regiment were strung along the road for miles and it took some of them 24 hours to make the trip. On July 26th we boarded a freight train at Hagerstown for Indianapolis, Ind. When we reached Greencastle, Pa, the citizens gave us a lunch. A beautiful young lady gave me a cigar to smoke after lunch. She was so nice and beautiful I could not resist smoking it in fond memory of her and her beauty. Right there was where and how I commenced smoking. I am still smoking, I suppose in fond memory of the girl and her beauty. I can give no other tangible reason. She doubtless thought she was doing me a kindness when she gave me the cigar but I must reverently say, curse the result.

We reached Indianapolis July 29th and were mustered out of the first three month's service at Indianapolis, Indiana, August 7, 1861. I had re-enlisted for three years before returning to Indianapolis and when I arrived there I found a number of my neighborhood boys had enlisted in my company for three years service. When the regiment was first organized, my company was made and designated "Company G." As soon as I reached Indianapolis the men of Company C of the 18th Indiana Regiment came to see me and

---

[42] John E. Cook of Connecticut joined John Brown in Kansas, then moved to Harper's Ferry in 1858. He married a local woman in April 1859, and participated in Brown's failed attempt to seize the US Arsenal later that year. He escaped capture in Harper's Ferry but was eventually caught, tried, and convicted of murder and inciting a slave insurrection. He was executed on 16 December 1859. Durham describes Jefferson Rock, a formation that still stands in Harper's Ferry, as the scene of Cook's wedding. No evidence could be found to support Durham's version of the marriage ceremony. After Virginia's secession in 1861, however, marriages were performed in the Potomac River (claimed by Maryland) to make the bond legal in the United States. Some couples extended a stout plank across the river and performed the ceremony while standing on the plank to accomplish the same purpose (Stephen B. Oates, *To Purge this Land with Blood: A Biography of John Brown* [Amherst: University of Massachusetts Press, 1970] 218–19, 275, 288–302, 328). Further information on Cook may be found in Richard J. Hinton, *John Brown and his Men* (New York: Funk and Wagnalls Co., 1894) 466–67, 474–75 and Oswald Garrison Villard, *John Brown, 1800–1859: A Biography Fifty Years After* (New York: Alfred A. Knopf, 1943) 680–81.

insisted on me taking the 1st Lieutenancy of their company. In the first formation of companies the men of the company were allowed to elect their officers and as my old boyhood chum, Brent Davis, belonged to that company, he got the company to elect me their First Lieutenant.[43] But I was so wedded to my own regiment that I declined the office. Many of the boys of our regiment accepted commissions in other regiments at the end of the first three month's service and some of them came out at the close of the war Brigadier Generals. I, perhaps, could have done the same thing had I accepted the position offered me and had had the same ambition for office that some of them had. I had an ambition to shoot at the rebels as I thought I could do more personal execution that way than I could by carrying a sword and ordering the other fellows to shoot, but I found later on in the war that a brave officer could cause more punishment to the enemy than any one private could with his gun. I never asked for a promotion or an office during the war. The one thing that held me back was my feeling the lack of education. I knew my education was deficient and that caused me to lack confidence in myself that I really should have had. I naturally took to military subjects and I learned the tactics readily and delighted in the drills and maneuvers.

When we returned to camp at Indianapolis I was put to drilling the new recruits—in fact I had to drill the new officers of the company. It was the custom in raising recruits to give offices to those who recruited the most men for a certain company. Before we returned from the three month's service there was an officer from each company sent home to recruit his company for the three years' service. He would select a man well acquainted with his section of the country, or his town, and offer him an office if he would recruit so

---

[43.] Probably Corporal Samuel B. Davis of Company C, 18th Indiana Infantry. A resident of Vermillion County, Davis was mustered into service on 16 August 1861. He was mustered out of service at an unspecified date (Terrell, *Report of the Adjutant General,* [Indianapolis: Samuel M. Douglass, 1866] vol. 4, 376; [Indianapolis: Alexander H. Conner, 1868] vol. 8, 42).

many men for his (the officer's) company. This fellow, being anxious for an office, would work hard among the boys with whom he was acquainted, to get them to enlist. This was a good scheme for recruiting but it was not good policy for the army, for all the men of the three months' service who re-enlisted, were well drilled and to put an officer over them who they knew did not know how to "right face" did not have a good influence. Many like myself had to drill the officers that were to command them. Milt Clark and Jessie [sic] Custer recruited most of the men for my Company "G" and in the formation of the company for the three years' service, Gum Carr retained his position as Captain. Dave Knox, who was our First Lieutenant, did not re-enlist and John F. Cavin [sic], who was our Second Lieutenant, was made First Lieutenant.[44] Milt Clark was made Second Lieutenant and Jessie Custer First Sergeant. There were five Sergeants in the company and I was appointed Fourth Sergeant. I did not like Milt Clark from my first sight of him. I knew he had been promised a Lieutenancy by the recruiting officer and I went to Col. Wallace and protested against him appointing Clark as Lieutenant. I told Wallace I did not think Clark was the man for the place and that I considered him a numbskull and a coward. Wallace replied "No, Tom, you are mistaken, why I know he struck a fellow in Crawfordsville one day with his fist and broke the fellow's jaw." But

---

[44] Milton Clark of Crawfordsville IN was commissioned a second lieutenant in Company G on 31 August 1861, and was promoted to first lieutenant that November. He resigned in August 1862. Jesse Custer of Boone County IN became a second lieutenant in November 1861, was promoted to first lieutenant in August 1862, and to captain of Company F in September 1863. John F. Caven of Crawfordsville IN was commissioned second lieutenant in Company G (three months) in April 1861, was advanced to first lieutenant in the three years' 11th Indiana in August, and finally to captain of Company G in November. He served until mustered out in November 1864 (Terrell, *Report of the Adjutant General*, vol. 2, 30, 80–81). David R. Knox is not listed in the *Indiana Adjutant General's Report* as an officer in Company G, but according to another source was commissioned a second lieutenant in the regiment on 25 June 1861 (US Adjutant General's Office, *Official Army Register of the Volunteer Force of the United States Army*, vol. 6 [Washington, DC: Adjutant General's Office, 1865] 418).

later on I think Wallace found out, as I did, that the fisticuffs and bully bluffers were as a rule the worst cowards in battle.

When I got back to Indianapolis I found many troops mobilized there—recruiting, organizing and drilling—preparing to go to the front. The city, by this time, was full of fakers of all kinds, such as three-card monte, the shell game, the string game, and many other fakes by which they relieved the innocent and unsophisticated boys, who had just left the farm, of all the cash their parents had given them when they left home. "The Wandering Jew" with his cheap "pure gold" watches and jewelry was greatly in evidence. They had rich picking for a while but the boys soon got onto their racket and when one would appear in camp with his bogus jewelry, you would soon hear some fellow yell "here is a Christ killer," and that was the signal for the boys to gather in. They would take charge of mister Jew, confiscate his jewelry and give him such punishment that he would never want to return to camp again. Often they would give him the "blanket bounce" which was done in this way: they would get an army blanket with a stout man holding each corner and would throw mister Christ killer on the blanket, bounce him high up in the air, then lower the blanket so Mr. Jew would bump on the ground. He would no sooner strike the ground than up would go the blanket again and they would bounce him in this manner until he would barely be able to get out of camp. Then they would tell him to "git" and you can be sure he "got." Often some fellow who had been especially soaked in buying a ten cent brass watch for a fine gold one at a gold price, would knock Mr. Jew down and give him a few kicks as a personal satisfaction.

One night while I was sleeping in a tent with some of the recruits from my neighborhood, an old Austrian stole the blankets off some of the boys. It woke me and I saw him take the blankets so I woke the boys up and told them of the theft and that they had better go capture the thief. They crawled to the front of the tent and looked out but were afraid to follow the thief as they saw he wore a belt with a sword bayonet hanging by his side. They laid down again and I asked them why they did not go capture him. They said we will get him in the morning. I told them they would play thunder getting him in the morning. I saw they were afraid to tackle him so I took an old empty Navy I had and went out and hunted for the fellow. I soon found him with an armful of blankets he had stolen from the recruits. I hid behind a tent until he passed by. As he did so I sprang out and shoved my old Navy in his face, cocked it and ordered him to hand me the sword bayonet. I then marched him to my tent and the boys identified their blankets and I could hardly keep them off the thief, but I told them as they were too cowardly to tackle him before I captured him, they could not now while he was my prisoner. The fellow could have used me up with his sword bayonet had he known my revolver was empty but as it was dark he could not see through it and my bluff was a success. I guarded him the balance of the night and took him in the morning before Col. Wallace. I never had heard such scathing rebukes as Wallace gave him; he bemeaned him to everything he could think of and then told him if he was ever caught in camp again he could brand "thief" on him with a red hot iron and drive him out of camp. The Colonel complimented me very highly for capturing the thief.

While at Indianapolis we put in all our time drilling. I was kept busy drilling awkward squads, as those were called who could not catch onto the drill readily. Before we left Indianapolis I was sent down home to capture and bring back one of the boys who had deserted. I went by rail to Greencastle, thirty miles from home and there I hired a horse from my uncle, Dave Heath, who had married a half-sister of my mother's and who was a strong rebel sympathizer. He let me have a horse that I am satisfied he thought would kill me to ride. If such was his intention he was almost correct, for of all the horses I ever bucked, I never bucked such a man-killer before or since. I got home about four o'clock in the morning. I raised a window, went into the house, struck a light and sat down in front of the old fireplace. When I struck the light it woke my father and when he recognized me his greeting was "Hello Sally, where did you hail from?" I soon learned that the fellow I was looking for had gone to Kentucky. I stayed at home until about 9 o'clock that morning, then started back for Indianapolis as I was in a hurry to get back as the regiment was expected to leave there in a day or two.

Chapter 3

PADUCAH, HENRY, AND DONELSON

We were mustered into the U.S. Service for three years on August 31, 1861. We left Indianapolis, Indiana, for St. Louis, Missouri, on September 7th and reached St. Louis on the forenoon of the 8th. We went in freight cars to Alton, Ill., then by boat. We stayed that night in the old Benton Barracks; the next morning we went into camp just southwest of the city. There I saw, for the first time, General John C. Fremont, the old pathfinder, who was at that time in command of the Department of Missouri.[45] General Fremont was a small man, dark complexioned, with black hair, whiskers and eyes. He wore a long full beard, was quick and alert, had a fine military bearing and was of a dashing disposition. On September 10th we boarded a transport on the Mississippi River and went down river to Cairo, Illinois. When we got to Paducah we found a rebel flag floating over a large house—the finest house in town. It belonged to a wealthy old rebel aristocrat. General Smith had just let it "float."[46] We, immediately on landing, proceeded to tear it down. General Smith sent his bodyguard to arrest all who participated in the tearing down of the flag, as according to his idea of army regulations, it was done without orders from the

---

[45] John Charles Fremont (1813–1890), explorer, hero of the Mexican War, and Republican candidate for president in 1856, was appointed a major general in 1861 and given command of the US Western Department with headquarters in St. Louis. Fremont was blamed for two Union defeats in his department (Wilson's Creek and Lexington MO) and criticized for his order threatening death to all those found in arms against the United States and freeing the slaves of enemies of the Union. President Lincoln removed Fremont from command in November 1861 (Patricia L. Faust, ed., *Historical Times Illustrated Encyclopedia of the Civil War* [New York: Harper Collins Publishers, 1986] 291).

Commanding General and therefore was a high offense. When his bodyguard came to arrest us, Col. Lew Wallace formed his regiment in line of battle and told the guards to tell General Smith that he would not allow any of his men to be arrested for tearing down a rebel flag and that he would have to whip his regiment before he could arrest them. The general then ordered a couple of their regiments to arrest our regiment and they refused to do so. This was very humiliating to General Smith, he being an old regular army officer, but the rebel flag never again floated over that house as we had informed the owner we would tear the house down if it was raised again.[47]

My brother, John H. Durham who had just returned home from the Rocky Mountains in the fall of 1861, and my father visited me at Paducah in November. About the last of November I took typhoid fever. I did not think there was much the matter with me and I stayed in camp, did not go to see the doctor, but kept getting worse and finally got so weak I could not stand on my feet. Some of the boys finally took me to the hospital about the middle of December. They

---

[46] General Charles Ferguson Smith (1807–1862)graduated from West Point in 1825 and became a career army officer. In the fall of 1861 he was placed in command of the US District of Western Kentucky with headquarters at Paducah. Lew Wallace described him as "the best all-around officer in the regular army—a disciplinarian, stern, unsympathetic, an ogre to volunteers, but withal a magnificent soldier of the old school of Winfield Scott" (Lew Wallace, *An Autobiography*, vol. 1 [New York: Harper and Bros., 1906] 338; Ezra J. Warner, *Generals in Blue: Lives of the Union Commanders* [Baton Rouge: Louisiana State University Press, 1964] 455–56). At least some enlisted men in the 11th Indiana agreed with Wallace. One soldier referred to Smith as "our worthy commander," and a polite gentleman, very sociable and companionable. "He looks like a soldier," the Hoosier continued, "and I think will yet prove himself to be such" (*Indianapolis Daily Journal*, 28 December 1861). Like Winfield Scott, Smith held officers personally responsible for the conduct of their troops and strove to protect the property of Paducah's citizens (*Indianapolis Daily Journal*, 19 September 1861).

[47] Although Wallace downplays this event in his autobiography, other evidence tends to support Durham's recollections regarding the serious nature of the incident, if not the exact details. According to other accounts, a Paducah citizen named Woolfolk occasionally flew a Confederate flag from his house, and General Smith refused to order him to take it down. On 25 November 1861, three or four officers of the 11th then took a Union flag to Woolfolk's house, and informed Mrs. Woolfolk that they intended to fly it from the home. She requested time to send for her husband, and in the interim sent word of the encounter to General Smith. The general came to the Woolfolk home and ordered the Hoosiers away.

laid me on the floor in the office room of the hospital. Rockwell, the hospital steward, was standing at a high writing desk. He was a very large man, raw-boned and with large white greasy eyes that looked more like a sheep's eyes than human, and I despised him at first sight. He finally looked down at me and in a very gruff manner asked "What is the matter with you?" I told him I did not know and he then said "There is nothing the matter with you, there are plenty of men in camp doing duty who are much worse than you are. You have just got a little touch of jaundice. I have no room for you here, you can go back to camp." To accuse me of playing sick or as we called it "playing old soldier," was the highest insult that could possibly be given me, as I do not think there was anyone who could have a greater contempt for a soldier who was playing sick than I had. His insinuation that I was not sick, but simply playing it to get rid of camp duty was too much for me. I had generally carried a Navy and a knife on my belt and as I went down for them I found I did not have them and I thought I would tear the villain to pieces anyhow.[48] When I found I was too weak to get to my feet my reason left me in an instant and I

After the Indiana officers returned to camp, their men became excited, and soon the whole regiment was marching to the home, led by the regimental band playing "The Marseillaise." The Hoosiers then hoisted the Stars and Stripes from the house as the band played "The Star Spangled Banner," "Yankee Doodle," and other patriotic airs. Following the ceremony, the men quietly dispersed and returned to camp. Lew Wallace witnessed the affair on his way to Smith's quarters, but did not interfere with the flag raising and ordered his men back to camp. The incident was not without bloodshed, however. Apparently after the first attempt to raise the flag, Lieutenant J. T. Price, one of Smith's aides, returned to the scene, condemned the act, and after an argument with Captain Frederick Knefler, struck the captain in the face. Knefler responded by knocking Price into the mud. Wallace then intervened and saved Price from further harm, as cries of "kill him" could be heard, one soldier tried to slash Price with a knife, and another kicked the helpless aide. The "Stars and Stripes" remained, but Smith issued a general order denouncing this violation of good order and discipline. Durham was probably sick at this time and did not take part in the event, and merely repeated rumors he heard about the occurrence. The Chicago *Tribune*, St. Louis *Daily Missouri Republican*, and other papers devoted space to the incident (Frank Moore, *The Rebellion Record*, vol. 3 [New York: G. P. Putnam and D. Van Nostrand, 1861–1868] 89, 418–19; *Indianapolis Daily Journal*, 30 November, 3 December, 4 December, 5 December, 12 December, 30 December 1861; Robert E. Morsberger and Katharine M. Morsberger, *Lew Wallace: Militant Romantic* [New York: McGraw-Hill, 1980] 64–65).

[48] Not everyone felt the same way about Hospital Steward Rockwell. A soldier identified only as "H.B.H." complimented him as "our most efficient Hospital Steward" (*Indianapolis Daily Journal*, 7 June 1862).

was delirious for more than two weeks. After I came to my reason I was told that in my delirium I was trying to kill that pirate of a steward. The only rational moment I had in that more than two weeks of delirium was when I seemed to open my eyes as from a sleep and saw the surgeon and ward master bent over my cot looking at me, and I remember the surgeon saying to the ward master "Move this man to the best ward in the hospital for it will be a hard matter to save him." I think that must have been soon after I was taken to the hospital.

Soon after we got to Paducah, Col. Wallace was promoted to Brigadier General and he promoted Dr. Thomas Fry, my father's old friend, to the position of Brigade Surgeon and Dr. Thompson, the first assistant surgeon, was promoted to surgeon of the regiment.[49] It was Thompson who attended me while I was in the hospital. He was a very kind and sympathetic man and I learned afterward that when he learned how that goggle-eyed steward had treated me, he gave him a fearful raking and came near having him reduced to ranks. But that was not all of the cussedness of that steward. When my folks at home found out I was sick, they sent me a box of provisions such as a convalescent could eat, including dried and canned fruits, butter, maple syrup, honey and many other delicacies. When the box came to the hospital that pirate of a steward took charge of it, opened it, and never let me know a thing about it but ordered the Sisters of Charity, who waited on the sick and prepared the food for the hospital, to put all the provisions my folks had sent me on his table

---

[49] Wallace's commission as brigadier general of volunteers was dated 3 September 1861. Because of the promotion, Wallace assumed command of a brigade consisting of the 11th and 23rd Indiana and 8th Missouri, while Lieutenant Colonel George McGinnis was commissioned colonel of the 11th Indiana (Wallace, An Autobiography, vol. 1, 345–46). Dr. John C. Thompson of Terre Haute IN was commissioned surgeon of the 11th and served until his resignation in December 1862 (William H. H. Terrell, Report of the Adjutant General of the State of Indiana, vol. 2 [Indianapolis: W. R. Holloway, 1865] 76).

and not to let me have any of them. But as I did not groan and take on like I thought I was going to die, the Sisters seemed to take a liking to me and told me what the steward had done.[50] All I got of the provisions sent me from home was what little the Sisters could steal out and bring to me unbeknown to the steward. I will say right here that if my gentle readers think I did not lay for an excuse to kill that villain, they are off. I was told I did not take a particle of nourishment for over two weeks and they kept me alive by giving me brandy. The wives of General Lew Wallace and General George F. McGinnis visited me at the hospital quite often and were very kind me—all of which I appreciated after the treatment of that brute of a steward.[51] I was discharged from the hospital the last of January 1862. I was very thin and weak and hardly able to mope around.

On the fifth of February the regiment embarked by boat to go up the Tennessee River. As I was thin and weak the officers did not want me to go but I was determined to go with my regiment. On February 6th we disembarked on the west bank of the river a little below Fort

---

[50] Dr. Fry took over Paducah's Old School Presbyterian parsonage as a hospital for the 11th Indiana. The "commodius" two-story building had five rooms and a kitchen on the first floor, and two large rooms and one small room above, capable of accommodating thirty patients. Fry reported that he had hospital stores in abundance, all the hospital attendants necessary to wait on the patients, plus two of the Sisters of Charity assigned to the regiment. By late November 1861, the 11th had thirty-two men in the hospital, but only three of them were seriously sick (*Indianapolis Daily Journal*, 20 November, 25 November 1861). For an earlier (mid-October) and far different view of the Paducah hospital situation, see the letter of Lew Wallace to Susan Wallace, dated 5 October 1861 (copy in files of Ben Hur Museum, Crawfordsville IN).

[51] George Francis McGinnis (1826–1910), a Mexican War veteran and hat manufacturer in Indianapolis, enlisted in the 11th Indiana when the war began. McGinnis served as lieutenant colonel in the three-month unit and lieutenant colonel and colonel of the three-year regiment. He performed well at Fort Donelson and Shiloh and was made a brigadier general of volunteers in April 1863. After he led a brigade of the 13th Army Corps in the Vicksburg Campaign, McGinnis was a brigade and division commander in the US Department of the Gulf and Department of Arkansas before the war ended (Warner, *Generals in Blue*, 299–300). The *Indianapolis Daily Journal* noted that McGinnis was "an especial favorite among military men, and has the enviable reputation of knowing more about tactics than any officer of the volunteer service." One soldier agreed that "He is acknowledged to be the best drill-master that is in the service from Indiana," and "Our old Wellington," suited for a difficult march, handling a regiment, or storming a battery (*Indianapolis Daily Journal*, 16 May 1862).

Henry and Fort Heiman.[52] Fort Henry was on the east bank of the river and Fort Heiman was right opposite on the west bank. Our gun boats were bombarding the forts at Henry. We marched on Fort Heiman and in doing so we had to wade across a bay where the icy water came up to our armpits. We put the bayonets on our guns, hung the cartridge boxes on the bayonets and held our guns above our heads to keep the powder dry. We got close to the fort before we were discovered by the enemy and we charged the fort. There was a regiment of Alabama troops in the fort and it was a new regiment which had seen no service. They had company cooks and tables that would accommodate the whole company and they had their grub all on the tables and ready to partake of it when we charged them. They "skiddaddled" with very little show of resistance. Even though they were swift on foot, we perhaps could have captured many of them had we not stopped to eat their dinner for them before it got cold. In fact we felt too kindly toward them for preparing such a nice dinner for us to do them much bodily harm. The other troops outside the fort retreated when they saw that those in the fort had stampeded. It was not very long after we captured Fort Heiman until the fleet silenced the batteries at Fort Henry, then the marines and land forces stormed the forts and took them, capturing General Tilghman and his staff and about 90 men, also all the armament of the fort, including ammunition and provisions.[53]

---

[52] The 11th Indiana left Paducah KY on 5 February aboard the steamer *Aleck Scott* and landed near Fort Heiman the next morning at 9 A.M. The regiment arrived at the fort at 3 P.M. (Janet B. Hewett, ed., *Supplement to the Official Records of the Union and Confederate Armies*, vol. 16, serial 28 [Wilmington NC: Broadfoot Publishing Co., 1995] 133). Fort Heiman was an earthwork fort located directly across the Tennessee River from Fort Henry and named for Colonel Adolphus Heiman of the 10th Tennessee Infantry.

[53] Confederate Brigadier General Lloyd Tilghman led the hopeless defense of Fort Henry, and surrendered twelve officers, sixty-four fighting men, and twelve convalescents (Benjamin Franklin Cooling, *Forts Henry and Donelson: The Key to the Confederate Heartland* [Knoxville: University of Tennessee Press, 1987] 110).

My regiment was in the 1st Brigade, 1st Division of the 13th Army Corps. General Lew Wallace commanded the brigade, General C.F. Smith the Division and another general the Corps.[54] General U.S. Grant was in command of all the troops in this expedition. General C.F. Smith's division was landed on the west bank of the river and the 2nd Brigade moved to the rear of Fort Heiman and our 1st Brigade moved directly on the fort. General Grant landed all the other troops on the east bank to assault Fort Henry. In all we had nearly 17,000 troops. As the waters were very high the troops had great difficulty in reaching Fort Henry. There is a bend in the river at Henry so the guns in the fort, or what were called the "water batteries" had direct range down the river. There were only 2800 soldiers in Fort Henry but there was a large reinforcement from Fort Donelson halted a couple of miles out from Henry.[55] General Tilghman sent his garrison to the rifle pits surrounding the fort. When our troops attacked them they retreated to the reinforcements from Donelson. General Grant, seeing the situation and the necessity for quick movement on his part in order to capture the fort before the reinforcements from Donelson could reach it, ordered all the troops on either side of the river and also the gunboats, to move at once up the river and attack the forts. Below Henry the ground was low and covered with water, making it very difficult for the land troops on the east side of the river to approach Fort Heiman, which was located on high ground overlooking Henry. There were seven-

[54] Actually Grant's army was not formed into corps at this time. The 11th Indiana was a part of Colonel Morgan L. Smith's Fifth Brigade in Brigadier General Charles F. Smith's Second Division (*Official Records*, ser. 1, vol. 7, 168–69).

[55] Reinforcements from Fort Donelson did not assist the Fort Henry garrison. In his memoirs, Ulysses S. Grant noted that he wished to commence operations against Fort Henry as soon as possible before the enemy could reinforce it, that it was natural to suppose that additional troops would be sent to the fort, and that "strong reinforcements from Donelson halted some miles out" from Henry. Durham undoubtedly included this information after reading Grant's memoirs (Ulysses S. Grant, *Personal Memoirs of U. S. Grant*, vol. 1 [New York: Charles L. Webster & Co., 1885] 290–91).

teen guns mounted at Fort Henry. Captain William Porter commanded our fleet of gunboats and he attacked the fort at close quarters. It was a grand but wicked looking fight between the fleet and the fort. I was where I had a good view of the engagement. All of the boats were struck many times but none except the Essex was very badly disabled. A shell punctured the boiler of the Essex, exploding it and killing and wounding forty-eight of her men.[56] I saw where a queer thing happened in the fort—a shell from our gunboats penetrated the muzzle of one of the guns in the fort, exploded in the gun and burst the gun to atoms, killing a number of the enemy. It was a sickening sight to see the brains, hair and fragments of human flesh scattered all around where the explosion took place.

Fort Donelson is situated on high bluffs on the west bank of the Cumberland River east of Fort Henry. These forts were separated by a watershed twelve miles across. The purpose of these forts was to prevent us from penetrating the enemy's country by either the Tennessee or Cumberland Rivers and was of great importance to the enemy. Our troops followed the retreating foe from Henry to Donelson, capturing two cannon and a number of stragglers. Our regiment remained at Fort Heiman as guards.[57] The night of the sixth, after the fall of the two forts, I was on duty as officer of the guard. I had charge of the camp vacated by the new Alabama regiment and as that regiment had just arrived, fresh from home, they

---

[56] Actually Captain Andrew Hull Foote commanded the flotilla that bombarded Fort Henry. Commander William D. Porter was aboard the *Essex*. Ten men were killed, twenty-three were wounded, and five missing after a Confederate round struck the ship's boiler (Cooling, *Forts Henry and Donelson*, 105–106).

[57] Confederate Lieutenant Colonel J. F. Gilmer, chief engineer of the Western Department, reported that a 24-pounder gun burst during the attack on the fort, killing three men, while a 42-pounder cannon prematurely discharged and killed three others. In addition, a 32-pounder cannon was struck by Federal fire and the gunners were disabled. Durham may have inspected any of the three (*Official Records*, ser. 1, vol. 7, 134).

were well supplied with comforts.[58] I found feather beds, trunks and almost everything one could imagine. I took an inventory of all they had. I opened all the trunks (with one key) and found hundreds of pictures of the girls the boys had left behind and hundreds of letters from the loving girls to the brave boys who had gone to fight Yanks. I gathered up more than a thousand of these letters and pictures for the purpose of furnishing amusement in camp. Each company of the regiment had just drawn a box of "cleavers" or knives, that were not yet opened. I opened them. These cleavers or knives were from a foot and a half to two feet long with a handle at one end and a sharp point at the other and had a very sharp edge; they looked much like the old fashioned corn knife. In the early part of the war the rebels furnished most all their troops with these large knives, with which they expected to mow the Yankies [sic] down in large swaths, but they soon found what a useless and foolish weapon it was. After the war a rebel lieutenant explained it very aptly to me. He spoke of how proud he was when the big knife was issued to him and how he was certain he could chop the Yanks down by the dozens—he could almost see them piled waist high around him. But he said that he found after his first battle that it was too close to get to the Yanks to suit him when he got within gunshot, much less being close enough to hew them down with his big knife or cleaver. All their troops threw these cleavers away after their first fight. I shipped an officer's trunk home that we captured at Fort Heiman, filled with a lot of trophies and have always regretted that I did not put one of these cleavers in it to keep as a relic of a rebel folly. The trunk I 'borrowed' from the rebel officer and shipped home is beside me now.

---

[58] Probably the 27th Alabama Infantry under the command of Colonel A. A. Hughes. On February 5, the regiment evacuated Fort Heiman and withdrew across the Tennessee River to Fort Henry (ibid., 138, 148–50).

A few days after the fall of Henry and Heiman, Grant moved the troops that were on the east side of the river toward Fort Donelson. He would have moved on Donelson immediately after the fall of Henry but he wanted the fleet of gunboats to act in conjunction with him at Donelson. Grant sent some of the gunboats up the Tennessee River to burn and destroy the bridge of the Memphis and Ohio Railroad which was across the river. These boats had to return, go down the mouth of the Tennessee River, then up the Ohio River to the mouth of the Cumberland, then up that river to Donelson. Some of the boats arrived below the fort on the evening of February 12th and Grant arrived on the same evening with his land forces. On the 13th the gunboats engaged the batteries of the fort at long range while Grant was getting his troops in position around the outer works of the enemy. At this time Grant had only 15,000 soldiers, while the enemy had 21,000 in their entrenchments. There was nothing more than a few hot skirmishes on the 13th while our men were taking a position as near as possible to the enemy's works. On the 14th a part of a division was ordered to charge a battery on the rifle pits that had been annoying. This was done without orders from General Grant and was repulsed with heavy loss. When Grant started to Donelson he left 2500 troops under General Lew Wallace to guard Forts Henry and Heiman. We received orders from General Grant on the night of the 13th to move at once to Donelson. We reached our line of battle near Donelson on the afternoon of the 14th and took our position in the line. Our whole fleet arrived below the forts about the same time we arrived and they immediately engaged the forts at close range but the water batteries of the enemy were very formidable and disabled several of our boats, hitting some of them more than a hundred times. In the evening our fleet had to withdraw while the disabled boats floated down the river out of range of the enemy's guns. Fort Donelson was a well-selected, strategic point as it was on a very high bluff on the west side of the river and was impregnable so far as an attack from the fleet was concerned. On Thursday, the 13th of February, 1862, our regiment went on a reconnoissance [sic] sout[h]west of Fort Heiman. We were gone all day and had a hard march. We got back to camp about dark—the temperature that day was mild and just before we reached camp it began to rain and then to snow and by midnight it was clear with a regular blizzard blowing. I have never seen a Kansas blizzard that could turn so cold in so short a time. It was about 10 o'clock when we had finished our supper and turned into our bunks for sleep. About midnight the "long roll" was sounded, calling us to arms.[59]

As I have said, we were camped at Fort Heiman on the west bank of the river. There was a bayou between us and the boat landing and the water in the bayou was too deep for our artillery to cross so we had to carry logs and build a bridge across the bayou for our artillery to cross on. These logs were covered with sleet and snow. We would get large logs on our shoulders, half of us with the right shoulder under the log and the other half with the left shoulder under the log. To carry these large logs required as many men as could stand under the log and give room to walk by "lock step." With these logs we had to wade in the water which was up to our armpits and as soon as we would step out of the water, which was floating mush ice at the time, our clothes would freeze stiff as a board. We worked in the water until daylight before we got our bridge completed.[60] We then crossed the river to Henry and marched from there to Donelson twelve miles away, reaching there a little after noon on the 14th.

---

[59] The call to arms was not a complete surprise. A member of the regiment noted that reports of the fighting at Donelson "created the most intense excitement in our camp, and somewhat prepared us for what was to follow" (*Indianapolis Daily Journal*, 28 February 1862).

[60] One Hoosier described rain and hail, followed by a chilling rain, and the ground covered with a sheet of ice. "Amid the blinding, chilling sleet and storm," the soldier wrote, "we crossed the Tennessee" (ibid.).

That night we had to lie in line of battle near the enemy's outer works. We had to "sleep on arms," which means to lie in line of battle with all our clothes and accoutrements on and our guns in our arms, ready to repel an attack the instant we got to our feet. We had no tents and were not allowed any fire; we lay on the snow and frozen ground with our wet and frozen clothes that night. A snowstorm during the night brought 5 or 6 inches of snow and while we suffered much with the cold, we did not suffer so much after the snow covered us. With our suffering from the cold and the bombardment which was kept up all night, there was no sleep for us.

The next morning, Saturday, February 15th, the enemy tried to cut through our lines on our right. They made the sortie before daylight. Our front at that point was not properly picketed and the enemy came with such a dash that many of our men were killed with bayonets before they got on their feet, as this was such a surprise to our troops. Consequently, the enemy had great advantage, and although our soldiers formed as best they could and contested the ground bravely, at this point the enemy drove our line back for more than a mile. Our troops who were contesting this ground finally ran out of ammunition and could not stand against an enemy larger than their own strength and who had plenty of ammunition, so some of our men lost their heads and stampeded. It must have been about 9:00 a.m. when our brigade, consisting of the 11th Indiana and the 8th Missouri, under command of Colonel Morgan L. Smith of St. Louis, Mo., were ordered by General Lew Wallace to take the place of the troops that were being driven back.[61] We had already marched to

---

[61] As with any Civil War battle, there was some disagreement about when particular events occurred. Colonel McGinnis of the 11th claimed that the order to prepare for action was given about 1 P.M. It is quite likely that the 11th was readied for combat that morning, as Durham states, in response to a plea for help from Brigadier General John A. McClernand, whose troops were driven back by a Confederate attempt to break out from Fort Donelson early on February 15. It is reasonable to assume that the 11th actually became engaged about 1:30 that afternoon, although Wallace believed that his men fought from about 2 P.M. until 3:30 (Hewett, *Supplement to the Official Records*, vol. 16, ser. 28, 123, 133; *Official Records*, ser. 1, vol. 7, 177, 179, 234; Lew Wallace, "The Capture of Fort Donelson," *Battles and Leaders of the Civil War*, vol. 1 [New York: Thomas Yoseloff, 1956] 422–24). Hoosier H. B. Hibben noted that the regiment was drawn up in line of battle the entire day, but went into action about 3:30 P.M. (*Indianapolis Daily Journal*, 28 February 1862).

the right where the battle was raging. We now stripped for battle, piling our knapsacks, haversacks and overcoats (in battle a soldier is expected to carry only his canteen filled with water and his cartridge box filled with cartridges). We marched forward to take our position in line of battle in front of the enemy. We met hundreds of soldiers coming from the front, some with heads bleeding, some with broken arms dangling at their sides, others with a gun used as a crutch or walking stick and a broken leg dangling under them. As we would meet them they would say, "Oh boys, they will give you hell—they gave us hell." Nor was the scene made more encouraging by the ambulances dashing by us filled with dead and wounded, the blood flowing from the back end of the ambulances, while the blood-covered heads of the dead and wounded were bouncing up and down as the ambulance dashed at full speed over the rough ground.[62] My feelings at that time can be better imagined than I can describe them. We knew we were going to take the place of those who had been so badly mangled—we knew we were going to face an enemy flushed with victory—we knew some of us would be wounded and some killed and we knew not who they would be, and right here I wish to say that whenever a soldier boasts that he had no fear or dread in going into battle, he is a coward and a profound liar. I do not believe that a soldier ever lived who did not have a feeling of dread in going into battle. It may be called fear, but it is not a feeling of cowardice but is a natural human feeling under such dangerous and trying circumstances. I can say for myself that I never allowed anyone to excel me in doing my whole duty in battle. I would have allowed myself to be shot to pieces rather than show the white feather or shirked my duty. Death with me was far preferable. To be branded a coward, my personal pride, my pride as a soldier, my pride as an American and my interest in the cause I was fighting for, kept me from ever thinking of showing cowardice, no matter how great the

---

[62] H. B. Hibben of the 11th also reported meeting stragglers from the morning's fight (*Indianapolis Daily Journal*, 28 February 1862).

danger and yet I admit I always had a feeling of dread in going into battle. I also admit that during the excitement of battle one forgets his danger and that dread is gone.

We soon reached the point where General Lew Wallace was sitting on his bald-faced charger, with field glasses to his eyes, viewing the enemy. He quickly turned to us and said, "Now boys the enemy has driven our troops back nearly two miles. I depend upon you to take this ground back—by God you can do it. Go in and remember Buena Vista." By this time the bullets were whistling around our heads at a lively rate.[63] We were formed in line of battle and while doing so Colonel Morgan L. Smith, who was commanding the brigade, was sitting on his horse right in front of us smoking a cigar. A bullet cut the cigar off close to his mouth and he spit the stub out, took another cigar from his pocket and called to one of the boys to give him a match. He lit it with such coolness that it had a very quieting effect on the high-strung nerves of the boys.[64] As we moved forward the bullets came thicker and faster. I was a sergeant and it was my duty to keep the men of my company up in ranks. One fellow lagged behind. I urged him to get in ranks and when I told him he had to, he mumbled something of a rebellious nature and right then I flew into a rage. I threw my gun down on him and told him I would give him just one second to get in ranks or I would drop him right there. He sprang into ranks with no further comment. My anger settled my nerves.

When we got near enough to the enemy we charged them. They gave way, then they rallied and made another stand. We dropped flat on the ground (this was our Zouave tactics) and we crawled forward on our bellies, not firing a shot, letting the enemy shoot over us until

---

[63] For a lengthy discussion of Wallace's role in the battle, see James A. Treichel, "Lew Wallace at Fort Donelson," *Indiana Magazine of History* 59/1 (March 1963): 3–18.

[64.] This story is corroborated in Wallace, *An Autobiography*, vol. 1, 417.

they thought we had retreated and then slacked their fire; then we would spring to our feet, give them a volley and at them with bayonet.[65] The fact of us crawling toward them while they were firing surprised them and when we gave them the volley and charge so close to them they did not understand our tactics. They would fall back when we would charge, then they would rally and make another stand; we would again drop to the ground and crawl toward them. We kept these tactics up until we drove them back into their works. We halted on a ridge about two hundred yards from their rifle pits.[66] All between this ridge and their works was filled with abatis. This consisted of trees cut and felled with the tops pointing outward from the forts, the limbs sharpened so an enemy assaulting their forts would get stuck on these sharp points, thereby impeding their progress and giving those in the forts more time in which to resist the assault. Often barbed wire stretched in front of forts is used as abatis.[67] When on this ridge we were in full view of the enemy works and in range of their cannon. They immediately opened on us with their artillery. They had good range on us and were tearing the ground up where we lay at a fearful rate with shell and solid shot.[68] I never was in a battle that there was not something occurred that was laughable.

While we were lying flat on this ridge and the shells were tearing up the earth around us, one of my company, Jake Buchanan, was lying with his head hidden behind an old stump. A shell struck the

---

[65] H. B. Hibben wrote that "This was a new thing to the rebels, and in which they were not prepared to imitate." Seeing that the Zouaves were relatively unharmed, the Confederates began to give ground (*Indianapolis Daily Journal*, 28 February 1862).

[66] Colonel McGinnis of the 11th Indiana believed that the regiment came within 500 yards of the enemy's entrenchments, while brigade commander Colonel Morgan L. Smith estimated 150 yards (*Official Records*, ser. 1, vol. 7, 233–34).

[67] Durham probably meant telegraph wire, as barbed wire had not yet been invented.

[68] H. B. Hibben also noticed that Confederate shot and shell killed several men in the regiment "even while they were lying flat upon their faces" (*Indianapolis Daily Journal*, 28 February 1862).

ground at the root of the stump and covered him with dirt and fragments of the stump. He then ran a few steps to the body of a dead soldier and crouched down behind the body. He had no sooner done so than another shell came and cut the body in two and plowed into the ground along Jake's side, covering him again with dirt and fragments of the body. By this time he was getting pretty well stampeded. He sprang up, then bobbed his head down behind an oak bush not larger than my finger to shield himself from a cannon ball, but there were dead leaves on the bush so he could not see the cannon very plain and he thought it all right. We soon dropped back under the crest of the ridge where we were out of range of the guns in the forts.[69] We lay there in line of battle all night with our bayonets fixed and with orders that if the enemy came out to wait until they got within 20 paces, then rise to our knees, give them a volley and at them with the bayonet and follow them into their works. We had to lie in the snow, the night was very cold, and we had had nothing to eat all that day. We had no blanket, no overcoat, nothing but a little Zouave jacket for a coat. We were not allowed to strike a match or speak above a whisper, nor were we allowed to rise to our feet—we had to lie still. The object was to surprise the enemy if they came. Of all the nights I have ever passed, this night of the 15th of February, 1862, during the battle of Fort Donelson, was the most horrible. Lying in the snow, the night fearfully cold, suffering from hunger, my clothes still wet and frozen from my half night spent in the mush ice and water of the Bayou, the suffering from the cold was almost beyond endurance. I thought I would certainly freeze to death.[70] My feet did freeze and I had absolutely no control over my lower jaw.

---

[69] Colonel McGinnis estimated this position was 800 yards from the Confederate fortifications (*Official Records*, ser. 1, vol. 7, 234).

[70] Colonel McGinnis agreed that the night was one of the coldest of the season, but unconvincingly stated that his men "submitted willingly and cheerfully and without a word of complaint" (ibid.).

My teeth chattered so I feared they would burst and added to all this suffering was the hideous groans of the hundreds of wounded and dying around me who were freezing to death and crying for help. I lay this night right where the onslaught of the morning had been made and I firmly believe I could have walked a half mile and stepped on either a wounded soldier or a dead body every step. It was appalling to see how thick they lay on the ground.[71] May the Lord grant that I shall never pass another such a night. There is something hideous in the cries of the wounded for help as they lay on the battlefield at night. It is worse than a nightmare and noone [sic] who has never heard them can ever imagine the horrors.[72]

The next morning at daylight (Sunday the 16th) we were in line of battle expecting every moment to receive orders to storm the forts. I must confess I did not feel like "storming" that morning and when in a few minutes we saw the white flag—the token of surrender—go up over the forts, I was so glad that I tried to throw my hat clear to the heavens and hoped it would lodge on the Great Throne, but it did not lodge as I finally saw it coming down with a shower of other hats that had been thrown with equal energy. We immediately marched into their works and took charge. I was so hungry that while marching in I espied a dead cow lying near where we were passing. I yanked out my old bowie knife and cut a chunk out of her thigh and ate it raw without salt or fire. Whenever I see a youngster snuffling

---

[71] Although Durham remained with his company and listened to the cries of the wounded, Colonel Morgan Smith assigned other men from the 11th Indiana to the disagreeable, nearly all-night task of carrying the Federal wounded to the rear (Ibid., 233). H. B. Hibben of the 11th recalled that the groaning and cries for help and water from the wounded continued through the night (*Indianapolis Daily Journal*, 28 February 1862).

[72] Although other brigades suffered heavy casualties at Fort Donelson, Colonel Smith's Fifth Brigade reported only eighty troops lost (eleven killed and sixty-nine wounded). The 11th Indiana reported four enlisted men killed and two officers and twenty-seven enlisted men wounded, accounting for thirty-three of the total (*Official Records*, ser. 1, vol. 7, 169).

over good food like he thought it not nice enough for him, I can hardly refrain from saying, "You 'dirty pup,' you never were hungry."

We captured about 15,000 prisoners at Fort Donelson and there had been over 20,000 of the enemy in Donelson but the night of the 15th, Generals Floyd and Pillow embarked on transports and went up the river to Nashville and took with them over 3,000 troops. General Forest [sic] escaped up the river bank with more than a thousand of the cavalry. General S. B. Buckner, the third in command at Donelson, did not flee from the wrath they saw coming as did Floyd, Pillow and Forest, but stayed with his soldiers and surrendered with them. I have neglected to state that late Saturday evening (the 15th), after we had driven the enemy back into their works, General C.F. Smith stormed their rifle pits to our left and succeeded in taking them and held his position that night inside their rifle pits. This made the capture of Donelson certain and forced the surrender of the forts. This is where General Grant got the name of "Old Unconditional Surrender." In answer to a request from General Buckner for a commission to arrange terms of capitulation, Grant answered that nothing but immediate and unconditional surrender would be accepted. I could give much more of the general history of this battle and surrender but will leave that for the historians of the war.[73]

On Sunday, the 16th, the day of the surrender, the weather moderated, the snow began to melt and in the afternoon it clouded up. As I had had no sleep since the night of the 12th except about two hours the night of the 13th, I was nearly dead for sleep and added to this the extreme exposure and excitement of the battle, I felt like I was about all in. That night we bivouacked in the enemy's works but we were ordered to sleep on arms as there was a report that General

---

[73] Forrest left the fort with about 500 cavalrymen and 200 infantrymen, while Floyd escaped with approximately 2,000 troops (Cooling, *Forts Henry and Donelson*, 205).

William Loring was returning with an army to raise the siege as they were not aware of the surrender. That night I lay in a little sunken place in the ground with my head on a chunk of wood for a pillow. When I woke up in the morning I felt myself all under water and slush except my face. It had rained in the night but I did not know that it had rained until morning and the water and melting snow had filled this sunken place full and as I was sleeping on my back my face was barely above water. I suppose the chunk I was using for a pillow saved my life as it kept my face above the water. Otherwise I did not doubt but what I would have been drowned before waking. Had anyone told me before I went into the army that I could sleep under a mush of snow and water as I did there, I would have called him a profound liar, but that convinced me that a man can be so dead for sleep that it is almost impossible to waken him.[74] •

On Monday, the 17th, we marched back to Fort Henry. My feet had thawed out and had swollen up so they burst my boots as I was marching. All the skin came off the bottom of my feet, so I had to finish the march on the raw flesh, and strange to say, after my feet got well, they were about two sizes smaller than they were before. I suffered from this fearful exposure more than most of the men on account of being very thin in flesh, having just recovered from a long spell of typhoid fever and the greatest mystery to me is why I did not take a relapse after all this exposure. We remained at Fort Henry until the 10th of March. I had to stay in camp all this time nursing my feet which in the meantime had gotten pretty well healed up and a brand new coat of skin on the bottoms. On the 10th of March we embarked on a boat and started up the Tennessee River. A large fleet of boats

---

[74] One soldier in the 11th believed that in addition to the regiment's losses in killed and wounded at Fort Donelson, exposure, hunger, loss of sleep, and hard marching through swamps had produced cases of ague, fever, bad colds, and rheumatism and added many to the sick list (*Indianapolis Daily Journal*, 6 March 1862).

went up the river at the same time, all loaded with soldiers and it made a grand sight.

On the 13th we disembarked at Crump's Landing on the west bank of the river.[75] That night we marched six miles out west from the river to a little town called Adamsville. This march was immemorable, for it poured down rain in torrents all night and it was so dark we could not see our hands before us except when there would come a flash of lightning. The soil of Tennessee is a red clay and very loose. A rain makes the mud very deep and there were deep gullies washed out on either side of the road. Some places those gullies were as deep as a man's head and not being able to see where we were marching, there was a constant splash from the soldiers falling into these gullies, and strange to say of soldiers, I heard some profane language when they would go headlong into these gullies. But the most profane profanity I heard was where a dead horse lay on a hillside across the road and in going down the hill I do not believe there was a soldier in the command who did not stumble over the old carcass and fall headlong into the mud.

We got to Adamsville some time before daylight. As the ground was covered with water I put a fence rail across the corners of a panel of fence and balanced myself well on the rail and took a nap. We were under light marching orders and we had neither blankets nor grub with us. After daylight I saw some geese in a field some distance away so I told a couple of the boys to go and borrow one of those geese and

---

[75] On the night of 12 March 1862, Lew Wallace moved his division by transport from Savannah to Crump's Landing in order to launch a raid on the Mobile and Ohio Railroad. The important rail line ran from Columbus KY to Mobile AL and was located a few miles west of the landing. While Union cavalry raided the railway, Wallace moved a brigade to the town of Adamsville. The 11th Indiana and Smith's Brigade remained at Linton's Farm, however, about three miles west of the river and two miles from Adamsville. When the cavalry successfully returned, Wallace reembarked his men at Crump's Landing on March 14. Shortly thereafter, however, Wallace landed his men again and established camps in the vicinity of the landing (Wiley Sword, *Shiloh: Bloody April* [New York: William Morrow & Co., 1974] 7–8, 41). Wallace's report of the railroad expedition may be found in *Official Records*, ser. 1, vol. 10, 8–16.

I would go to a farm house I saw about half a mile away and borrow a kettle to cook the goose in. I got a kettle and they had captured an old sturdy gander. We built a fire and just as the water got to boiling good the regiment was ordered to fall in ranks and we started back to Crump's Landing. We were hungry and did not propose losing our goose so we ran a stick through the bale of the kettle and carried it with us. After a while the command was halted and we started another fire, but again, just as our goose got to boiling good, we had to move on and this was repeated several times before we got back to the Landing; there we finishing [*sic*] cooking him. We had plenty of soup and we "borrowed" crackers from the boat and I think it was about the best meal I had during the war—at least we enjoyed it as we had had nothing to eat for more than 24 hours.

The next day, the 15th, we went into camp at Crump's Landing on the west bank of the Tennessee River in the State of Tennessee. There were three brigades in our division and Major General Lew Wallace commanding the division. Our brigade was stationed at the Landing, and the second was stationed at Adamsville, six miles out from the river and three miles west of Purdy.[76] There was nothing much of interest occurred while we were camped at Crump's Landing but I remember General Wallace teaching a couple of soldiers a lesson on foraging. At that early period of the war we had very strict orders against foraging. The officers did not favor the order but of course had to obey it, though they did all they could to keep from seeing any foraging going on. If they found a piece of beef, pork, mutton or a chicken in their mess chest, they never made any "roar" about it or used any great effort to find out who had put it there. But

[76] Actually, Wallace had positioned his Third Brigade (under Colonel Charles R. Woods) at Adamsville, about five miles from the Tennessee River, with the 1st Brigade (Colonel Morgan L. Smith) at Crump's Landing, on the river, and the Second Brigade (Colonel John M. Thayer) in between the other brigades at Stoney Lonesome. The remainder of Grant's army was encamped near Pittsburg Landing, about four miles south by river or six miles by road (Sword, *Shiloh*, 41).

one day a couple of soldiers came marching into camp with two hind quarters of beef hung on a pole on their shoulders. They passed right in front of General Wallace's headquarters and of course he could not help but see them. He ordered them arrested, made them hang the meat on the limb of a tree, and stand there for several days and keep the flies off the meat with brush. Finally, after the meat got to smelling too bad and he thought they had proper punishment, he had them dig holes and bury the meat. Then he had the guards bring them to his headquarters, where he proceeded to give them a gentle cursing and told them he hoped the next time they brought forage into camp they would have sense enough to not bring it right in front of his tent where he could not help but see them.

Chapter 4

SHILOH

Sunday morning, April 6, 1862, was a most beautiful and bright spring morning. The foliage on the trees was full size, hundreds of birds were singing and chattering in the branches of the trees and it was one of those rare and beautiful mornings that is so prone to lift one's thoughts from nature to nature's God. Every living thing seemed to be happy. Pittsburg Landing, or Shiloh, as it is now known, is six or seven miles up the Tennessee River from Crump's Landing. There the main body of Grant's army was camped. The advanced camps were two or three miles out from the Landing. The old Shiloh Church stood on a line with this advanced camp. About sun-up on this beautiful Sabbath morning of the 6th we heard the booming of cannon and the roar of musketry where the army was stationed up the river. It was the opening of the Battle of Shiloh.

We were eating our breakfast when we first heard the roar of battle. General Wallace immediately ordered the brigade to fall in ranks ready to march. I went with General Wallace to the wharf boat at the Landing and in a little while we saw General Grant coming up the river from Savannah on a transport. He was standing on the hurricane deck and as he passed us he saluted General Wallace and said, "Hold your troops in readiness to march at a moment's notice." General Wallace, returning the salute said, "My troops are in ranks now, ready to march." I was standing within a few feet of Wallace when Grant gave this order as he passed. We then went back to camp and waited for orders.[77] We stood there in ranks waiting for orders until about noon, when an officer, (I think a quartermaster) rode up and told Wallace that General Grant orders him to move his division immediately and join our extreme right. I was near Wallace at the time and heard the order given orally, but saw no written order given.[78]

On account of the main fighting being done around the old Shiloh Church, the battle was given the name of "Shiloh." A few days before this battle took place, General W.H.L. Wallace of Illinois, who commanded our extreme right at Shiloh Camp, and General Lew Wallace, had gone over the road running from Purdy, where our 2d brigade was stationed, which ran direct from Purdy to where W.H.L.

---

[77] On the morning of April 6, Wallace's Division was dispersed with the 1st Brigade (including Durham's 11th Indiana) at Crump's Landing, the Second at Stoney Lonesome, and the Third at Adamsville. Wallace, hearing the start of the Battle of Shiloh south of him, ordered his division to concentrate at Stoney Lonesome. The 1st and 2nd Brigades apparently united there by mid-morning. The 3rd Brigade, stuck in Adamsville because the roads were blocked by the rest of the division, did not leave until nearly 3 P.M. to join Wallace's march to the battlefield (US War Department, *The War of the Rebellion: A Compilation of the Official Records of the Union and Confederate Armies* [Washington, DC: Government Printing Office, 1880–1901] ser. 1, vol. 10, pp. 169–70, 175, 200; Lew Wallace, *An Autobiography*, vol. 1 [New York: Harper and Bros., 1906] 469; Albert Castel, ed., "The War Album of Henry Dwight," *Civil War Times Illustrated* 19/2 [May 1980]: 32–36).

[78] On the morning of April 6, Grant dispatched quartermaster Captain Algernon S. Baxter with a verbal order to find Wallace and direct him to march to the battlefield. Baxter put the order down on paper and found Wallace at Stoney Lonesome about 11:30 A.M. Wallace and one of his aides claimed that the order directed him to march to the army's right flank, not to Pittsburg Landing. Grant argued that the order sent Wallace to the Landing via the River Road, but also admitted that he was not certain just what orders Wallace received from Baxter. Unfortunately the original order was lost. Wallace began to march on the "Shunpike" Road about noon, after his men had finished dinner. A second courier, Illinois cavalry Lieutenant Frank Bennett, found Wallace about noon, before the march began, and delivered a verbal message for Wallace to hurry up, but did not specify the route he should take. Wallace himself wrote that the second messenger arrived about 1:30 P.M. while he was on the march. Some sources state that Bennett reported back to Grant and erroneously stated that Wallace would not march without written orders. A third officer, Captain William Rowley, was sent to deliver definite orders to Wallace, found him about 2:00 that afternoon, and told the general that Grant's forces had been driven back and that he should move to Pittsburg Landing. It is difficult to determine which courier Durham saw. The sequence of events would support the first courier, a quartermaster on Grant's staff, but he delivered written, not verbal orders. The second courier, on the other hand, while not a quartermaster, did deliver verbal orders to Wallace. If this was done at Stoney Lonesome, rather than on the march as Wallace believed, Durham likely saw Lieutenant Bennett (Wiley Sword, *Shiloh: Bloody April* [New York: William Morrow & Co., 1974] 218–20, 345; Wallace, *An Autobiography*, vol. 1, 465; *Official Records*, ser. 1, vol. 10, pp. 179, 185–86). Stacy D. Allen, "If He Had Less Rank: Lewis Wallace" in *Grant's Lieutenants: from Cairo to Vicksburg*, ed. Steven E. Woodworth (Lawrence: University Press of Kansas, 2001) 72-82.

Wallace's division was camped. This was a direct road from Purdy to our extreme right at Shiloh. The two Wallaces had this road repaired and had their cavalry go over it so they would be acquainted with the road. It was arranged between the two Wallaces that if one should be attacked, the other would go to his assistance over this road, which was the shortest and most direct road. Therefore, General Lew Wallace, being ordered to join our extreme right, naturally took this shortest and most direct road to that point, and he ordered his 3d Brigade to join him at Purdy. We, the 1st Brigade, on receiving the order from Grant, moved on "double quick" (a lively trot) to Purdy. We took the advance from Purdy to our right at Shiloh and moving on the double quick all the time.[79]

Just as we were crossing the Snake Creek bridge, which had formerly been the right of our army at Shiloh, a couple of orderlies overtook us with orders from General Grant to return and go up the river road, as the enemy had driven our line back below the Snake Creek bridge, and that to continue on that road would throw us in the rear of the enemy. In obedience to this order from Grant, we had to go back to Purdy, from there to Crump's Landing and then up the river. To show that General Lew Wallace was anxious to get into the battle with his division, it is only necessary to say that in this whole march of 20 miles or more, we went on a brisk trot all the time and at times it was so brisk it could more properly be called a run. We

---

[79] Durham is correct about the arrangement with General W. H. L. Wallace. Before the battle Grant's division commanders determined they would take the "Shunpike," leading from the Union Army's right flank to Lew Wallace's camps, rather than the River Road from Crump's to Pittsburg Landing, if the Confederates struck Wallace's isolated force. On April 6, therefore, Wallace used the prearranged route to send his men to aid the Union right. Durham is in error about the road leading to Purdy, a town far to the west of Wallace's encampment (Wallace, *An Autobiography,* vol. 1, 452; Sword, *Shiloh,* 345–46; Ulysses S. Grant, *Personal Memoirs of U. S. Grant,* vol. 1 [New York: Charles L. Webster & Co., 1885] 351–52.

reached our right flank at Shiloh about sundown and formed in line of battle on the extreme right of the Union forces.[80]

It is true, as Grant said in his order, that our forces had been driven or forced back below the Snake Creek bridge and to cross the bridge at that time would throw us in the rear of the enemy. General Lew Wallace had two batteries of field artillery and over five thousand veteran soldiers in his division. The soldiers all had implicit confidence in Wallace as their commander and if Grant had let Wallace go ahead we would have fallen on the enemy's rear and with Wallace's dash we would have stampeded the enemy and rolled their line of battle up and made the first day's battle a great victory for the Union troops. It is easy to see how this could have been done, for the enemy had all in their front that they could attend to without looking after an enemy in their rear. Furthermore, every foot we would have rolled the enemy's line up we would have had all the Union soldiers to join us who had been contesting that ground in front of the enemy, and it is very easy to see that the farther we rolled that line up, the greater the force we would have had to help us and the result would have been that we would have stampeded the whole rebel army at Shiloh on Sunday, the first day of the battle.[81]

---

[80] Captain Rowley, Grant's third courier, met Wallace on the "Shunpike" and informed the Hoosier of the seriousness of Grant's situation and the need to march to Pittsburg Landing, not to the army's right flank. Rather than reverse his troops, Wallace kept the division's original tactical arrangement by countermarching them back to a crossroads leading from the Shunpike to the River Road and Pittsburg Landing. On the way, at about 3:30, Wallace encountered a fourth and fifth courier (Lieutenant Colonel James McPherson and Captain John Rawlins) sent by Grant to speed the column. The extremely slow march, hampered by straggling, poor roads, and water crossings, resulted in Wallace reaching the battlefield just after 7:00 P.M. What should have been an easy, six-mile, two-hour march instead took more than seven hours and covered fifteen miles (Sword, *Shiloh*, 345–49, 380–81; Wallace, *An Autobiography*, vol. 1, 466–72; John W. Coons, *Indiana at Shiloh* [Indianapolis: William B. Burford, 1904] 31).

[81] Wallace made the same argument in his autobiography, but modern historians have concluded that had he continued his march on the Shunpike Road to try to gain the Confederate rear, he would have likely failed for a number of reasons (Wallace, *An Autobiography*, vol. 1, 467–68; Sword, *Shiloh*, 219).

All the regular army officers—the West Point graduates—stuck together. They were jealous of their laurels and when they saw their laurels were endangered by the volunteer officer who had entered the army from civil life, they all combined to clip his wings and see that he was placed where he could not take honors from them. Lew Wallace was not a West Point graduate but had entered the army from civil life and by reason of his bravery and generalship, he was rapidly promoted to the rank of Major General. This placed him where his success and popularity as a commander was a menace to the West Pointers, therefore, they determined to destroy his popularity. Some branded him as a coward, saying he took that road for the purpose of keeping out of battle. There was a great howl raised by these West Pointers against Wallace. They saw their opportunity to down him and they made the best of it. They claimed his first order from Grant was to take the river road and [he] had disobeyed orders by taking another, but that was soon proven to be false. They then said it was contrary to all military tactics for a small force to attack a large enemy in the rear as the large army always had a large reserve force that would capture the smaller force.

In this case, Albert Sidney Johnson [sic], commanding the rebel army at Shiloh, had absolutely no reserve, as is common in battle, but had every soldier in line, which would have made it easy for us to roll his line up. But even if he had had a reserve, we could have created such a stampede that even his reserve could not have checked it. Some claimed (I think at first Grant was of the opinion too), that Wallace had conceived the idea of taking this road, attack the enemy in the rear, stampede them and thereby make a great name for himself. But Wallace's bravery, dash and generalship at Donelson had made him not only popular with the soldiers but he received great praise from the Union people in the north. This made the West Pointers, or regulars, jealous and they were determined to down him.

So just before the evacuation of Corinth, Wallace was ordered to march his division across the country to Memphis, Tennessee, and soon after we got there he was relieved of his command and sent to command the Department of Ohio at Cincinnatti [*sic*], which was a nominal command and took him out of active field work at the front. They knew this would place him where he could not contest laurels with the regulars at the front.

General Grant at first claimed that Wallace was either ignorant of military tactics or was seeking to gain notoriety by attacking the enemy in the rear, either of which, according to the "books," was a grave violation of rules of war. In Grant's first article in the Century Magazine he said, "Later on in the war Wallace would not have taken the road he did," intimating that military tactics were then new to Wallace, but he learned by experience so that he would not have made the mistake in the latter part of the war. Wallace replied to this article by saying, "Later in the war Grant would have crossed General Buell's army at Crump's Landing and sent it over the road he (Wallace) took, and would have had Buell fall on the enemy's rear and bag the whole of Johnson's army, instead of crossing him at Pittsburg Landing as he did." There is no question but what Grant would have, later in the war, thrown Buell's army in the rear of the enemy. Grant as well as all the other generals at the beginning of the war had much to learn from experience.

I have always claimed that Wallace was very unjustly treated in this matter. As I stated above, the road Wallace took was the shortest and most direct road from his command to our right at Shiloh, and he did not know that our line had been forced back below the bridge. He did not expect to fall in the rear of the enemy, but would have fought him wherever he found him.

Grant, in his memoirs, completely exonerated Wallace of any blame because the widow of General W.H.L. Wallace had sent him

(Grant) a letter which she had found in the pocket of her husband's clothes, after he was killed at Shiloh, which explained fully the arrangements made between the two Wallaces to go to each other over this road in case of attack. This letter proved conclusively to Grant that Lew Wallace was in no way to blame for taking the road he did.[82] Yet it was too late, for Wallace had suffered the penalty for a military mistake that he did not make. I have gone into these details to show my readers that Wallace was wholly blameless, for I know there are historians who have blamed and censured him.[83]

As I have already said, we joined our right at Shiloh and took our position in line at about sundown Sunday the 6th. By this time the fighting of the day was about over, yet a cannonade was kept up all night. Early in the night a rain commenced to fall and continued the balance of the night. We lay all night in line of battle.

Some of our troops had camped where we were located and some of their tents were still standing. There was an officer's tent standing about 15 feet to the rear of my company. I concluded to step into this

---

[82] For a discussion of this letter, see Grant, *Personal Memoirs of U. S. Grant*, vol. 1, 351–52.

[83] For lengthy discussions of Wallace's controversial actions, see Grant, "The Battle of Shiloh," 468-69, Robert U. Johnson and Clarence C. Buel, "The March of Lew Wallace's Division to Shiloh," in *Battles and Leaders of the Civil War*, vol. 1 (New York: Thomas Yoseloff, 1956) 468–69, 607–10; *Official Records*, ser. 1, vol. 10, pp. 169–90; Irving McKee, *"Ben-Hur" Wallace: The Life of General Lew Wallace* (Berkeley: University of California Press, 1947) 53–57; Robert E. Morsberger and Katharine M. Morsberger, *Lew Wallace: Militant Romantic* (New York: McGraw-Hill, 1980) 87–94, 110–14; Larry J. Daniel, *Shiloh: The Battle That Changed the Civil War* (New York: Simon and Schuster, 1997) 256–61; Stacy D. Allen, "'If He Had Less Rank': Lewis Wallace," in *Grant's Lieutenants: From Cairo to Vicksburg*, ed. Steven E. Woodworth (Lawrence: University Press of Kansas, 2001); Harold Lew Wallace, "Lew Wallace's March to Shiloh Revisited," *Indiana Magazine of History*, 59/1 (March 1963): 19–30. A defense of Wallace's actions by a volunteer officer may be found in George F. McGinnis, "Shiloh," in *War Papers Read Before the Indiana Commandery, Military Order of the Loyal Legion of the United States* (Indianapolis: By the Commandery, 1898) 1–41. Wallace himself was "extremely sensitive" about the whole issue and continued to justify his actions on April 6 long after the war. In April 1894, for instance, he attended a reunion at Shiloh and traveled his division's route of march with some of his fellow officers, a surveyor, and some Confederate battle participants. Wallace felt that the endeavor justified his behavior during the march to the battlefield (*Crawfordsville* [IN] *Review* [14 April 1894]). Also see a lengthy April 1894 article from the *Indianapolis News* in the *Scrapbook of Articles on World War I and Civil War Reunions and Obituaries of Crawfordsville Residents, 1909–1919*, in the Crawfordsville (IN) Public Library, which includes a hand-drawn map and further information on Wallace's survey.

tent where I would be sheltered from the rain, knowing that if any disturbance occurred I could spring to my company at one bound. There was a trunk in the tent, and I lay down with my head close to the side of the trunk. I had not been there long until a shell from the enemy's guns struck the end of the trunk, tore it into fragments and threw them all over me. Being startled and stunned I sprang to the door of the tent with the idea of changing my location, but that instant the thought came to me that the fool gunner who seemed to have no respect for my comfort could not throw another shell in the same place and that I would be safer there than any place else, so I went back and lay down in the same place. My theory was correct, for no other shell went through the tent that night.[84]

As I was quite hungry, I began to skirmish around before daylight for something to eat. I found a sutler's tent nearby but the only thing I could find in it was a barrel of fine cut tobacco, so I shoved a handful of tobacco in my pocket and right there was where I started chewing tobacco and have been chewing ever since. That was one of the bad results of this battle.

As day was now breaking, I was ordered to take command of the right wing of the skirmish line. The regiment was standing in line of battle ready to advance and just before I advanced with the skirmishers, General Wallace rode along the line. Seeing me he said, "How are you feeling this morning Tom?" I answered jocularly, "I feel like I want to see my mother." He replied, "That is right, go in and remember the old folks at home." I have never believed in presentments but that morning before going into battle I was impressed with the feeling that something was going to happen to me. I did not feel that I was going to be killed but felt that some misfortune or suffering was going to be my certain lot in that battle. It impressed me so much

---

[84] Rather than Confederate artillery, it is likely that Durham was nearly killed by artillery fire from the Union gunboats *Lexington* and *Tyler* in the Tennessee River. Both ships lobbed rounds into the battlefield from 9 P.M. on the 6th until daylight the following morning (Sword, *Shiloh*, 374).

that I mentioned it to some of the boys, who laughed at the idea so I joined in the laugh and turned it off with a jest, but could not get rid of the feeling.

It is a peculiar fact that I have known of hundreds of instances where soldiers just before going into battle had a strong presentment that they were going to be killed, and would give their valuables to a comrade with the request that he send them to his people and it was almost invariably the case. They would be killed in the battle as they had had the presentment they would be. I have had them give me their valuables and the address of their parents just before going into battle saying, "I am going to be killed today." I would ask what made them think so and they would say, "I have a presentment," and I do not now remember of any who had that presentment or fixed idea in their heads that were not killed as they had thought they would be. Yet, with this feeling of certain death they would not flinch from duty and often fought with unusual bravery.

General Wallace opened the battle on Monday morning, April 7th. The battery in front of my regiment opened fire on the enemy a little after daylight. Our guns were answered by a rebel battery in their front and was carrying on a lively duel when I was ordered to take the right or First Platoon of my company and deploy them as skirmishers and advance and feel for the enemy. Those of us directly in front of our battery had to crawl on all fours so our guns could shoot over us. This was in an old field.[85] About one hundred and fifty yards in front of our battery was a fence running along the brink of a

[85] At about 5:30 A.M. on Monday, 7 April, Colonel McGinnis formed his regiment in line of battle along the Hamburg-Savannah Road and deployed skirmishers. After about an hour, McGinnis advanced the 11th about a half a mile to a hill within 500 yards of a Confederate battery, as troops from Colonel Preston Pond's Confederate brigade withdrew before him. After enduring heavy artillery fire for about two hours, McGinnis moved the regiment forward again. During this time different companies, including Durham's, were deployed as skirmishers. Durham claimed he was wounded about 7 A.M., probably somewhere in Jones Field, now preserved at Shiloh National Military Park (*Official Records*, ser. 1, vol. 10, p. 190; Coons, *Indiana at Shiloh*, 31; Thomas W. Durham pension record, RG 15, National Archives and Records Administration, Washington, DC).

hill that ran down to a wide gulch that lay between us and the ridge occupied by the enemy. This ridge held by the enemy lay in a half circle and the battery in front of us that was fighting with our battery was located in the center of the circle. When I reached the fence with my skirmish line, two batteries from the enemy opened on us. One was located on the right point of this half circle and the other on the left. These two batteries were shelling my line lengthwise. They had good range and the bursting shells were tearing the earth up all around us.[86]

Now as I had a battery in front of me, a battery in the rear of me and a battery on either side, all playing at the same time, saying nothing of the shells that were bursting around me, it made my location quite musical and as there was more force in this music than I cared for, I was watching our battery to see a chance for the skirmishers to jump over the fence without danger from our guns. I wanted to get the boys into the ravine in front, which was heavily timbered and I knew we would also be out of range of the enemy's guns. I finally saw an opportunity and ordered the boys to jump the fence. I sprang to my feet, placed my hands on the fence and was in the act of vaulting over it when a shell from the battery on my right exploded near me and a fragment struck me on the right hip and lodged against the bone. The piece that struck me was the metal that held the fuse in the shell and it was in the shape of a lap ring. It was whirling when it struck me and tore a large wound in the flesh. Some of the boys saw that I was wounded and offered to take me back to the regiment but I ordered them to move forward and get out of

---

[86] The only Confederate battery operating on this portion of the field was Captain William H. Ketchum's Alabama Battery, attached to Colonel Pond's brigade (Sword, *Shiloh*, 381–82, 457). It may be that Durham mistook separate sections of Ketchum's Battery for different units. Ketchum's Shiloh report may be found in *Official Records*, ser. 1, vol. 10, pp. 527–29.

range of the enemy's guns as soon as possible. I told them I would take care of myself.[87]

I commenced crawling back toward the regiment and soon some of the men saw me and came and carried me back in the rear of the regiment where the surgeon was stationed. He extracted the piece of shell, which he found lodged against the bone and then with a very serious look he asked me how I felt. The answer I gave him would hardly do for polite society so I refrain from repeating it, but after a hearty laugh at my reply he said, "By God you'll live—you are too game to die." My reply seemed to have impressed the old surgeon for after the war when I would meet him his first greeting would be, with a laugh, the same question asked over again. As I generally gave him the same answer I gave when he first asked the question, he delighted to ask the question in the presence of ladies, thinking I would forget their presence and give the same answer I did on the battle field. As soon as the surgeon had extracted the fragment of shell, he and a couple of soldiers put me on the Chaplain's pony and took me to the Landing. The surgeon went to all the boats at the Landing and tried to get them to let me be put on one of them. They all refused, saying that their boats were already crowded with wounded and not another man could be taken on. After the surgeon had been refused by the officers of all the boats he went to the captain of a boat who was standing on the gang plank and told the captain he was going to take me on board his boat. The captain protested saying that his boat was crowded with wounded and it was also a commissary boat and absolutely refused to take me on board. Whereupon, our surgeon, Dr. Thompson, ordered the boys to bring me on and then drew his

---

[87] Durham suffered a painful but not life-threatening wound. Statements in Durham's pension file note that a "deep and ugly wound" about two inches long and an inch wide was created to the rear of his right hip, just behind the hip joint. The wound was caused by an iron ring about one inch in diameter, an "open link of chain" thrown in by the bursting of the shell. The ring severely lacerated the muscle and apparently caused him pain for the rest of his life (Thomas W. Durham pension record, RG 15).

revolver and said to the captain of the boat, "This man cannot lie here and be trampled under foot like those men are and I am going to bring him on board this boat and you can stand aside or I will shoot you out my way." The captain stood aside.

I saw many disagreeable sights in the army but I think the one I saw when I was taken to the boat landing (Pittsburg Landing) that morning was the most revolting. There was a sand bar between the edge of the water and the river bank some 12 or 15 feet wide as I remember it now. This bar was more of a quick sand than otherwise for more than a hundred yards along the water's edge and was covered with dead and wounded. Some were buried clear under the sand with only a hand or a foot sticking out and men were walking over these bodies the same as if walking on a public road. I saw hundreds of men almost buried out of sight in the sand and were yet alive but were used as a pavement for men to walk on. The boys who were carrying me from boat to boat as the surgeon was trying to get a boat to take me on board had to walk on this road paved with men. It was this sight that caused Dr. Thompson to grow desperate and he proposed to do some killing before I should share their fate.

While such a sight looked inhuman, yet it could hardly be helped for the day before this many of our troops were stampeded and our line was forced back near the Landing. Comrades carried many of their dead and wounded to the Landing with the hope of getting them on a boat, so they would have some show of being taken home to their loved ones and when they found they could not get them on the boats, there was nothing to do but lay them on this sand bar. Another fact should be considered. Men in a stampede have not as much sense as an oyster—they would run over their mother-in-law and never see her. No, *I* never was in a stampede.

I was still 4th Sergeant at this time. My captain, John F. Cavin, was still at home wounded and our 1st Lieutenant was, as I have said, a "chuckle-head" with barely enough sense to right-face the company. He was despised by the company; his fellow officers did not like him and had no confidence in his bravery or ability. Colonel McGinniss [sic] had told me he would ask for his resignation as soon as the captain returned.[88] I think it was this lack of confidence in the lieutenant that caused Colonel McGinniss to order me to take command of the skirmish line. I was the first man wounded at Shiloh on Monday morning the second day of the battle.[89]

After Dr. Thompson had cleared the gang plank the boys carried me into the cabin of the boat. It was full of wounded soldiers and I barely had room to edge in on my side between other wounded soldiers. The whole cabin was a regular bedlam. Some were crying, some groaning, others cursing, and still others laughing; some were praying, while others were playing cards on the breast of a wounded comrade. I never was in a place before or since where there was such a variety of feelings displayed at the same time as there was there. It appeared that those having the least dangerous wounds were the ones who did the most howling. I lay on my left side on the bare floor without turning over or changing my position from Monday morning until Wednesday night.

When I was a boy I split the cap of my left knee and it has been weak ever since, and lying so long on my left side on that hard floor caused the knee to pain me so that I was sure it would give me the lockjaw. I never have suffered more intense pain than I did with that knee. When I was first placed on the boat I put my handkerchief in the wound and kept it damp with water from my canteen as long as it

---

[88] This was most likely Milton Clark, a resident of Crawfordsville who was commissioned a first lieutenant in Company G in November 1861, but who resigned in August 1862 (William H. H. Terrell, *Report of the Adjutant General of the State of Indiana,* vol. 2 [Indianapolis: W. R. Holloway, 1865] 81).

[89] The 11th Indiana lost eleven enlisted men killed and one officer and fifty men wounded, a total of sixty-two casualties, the highest number in Wallace's Division (*Official Records,* ser. 1, vol. 10, p. 102).

lasted. Some time in the night (Wednesday) I heard someone say that
there was a boat going down the river. I was determined to get on that
boat if possible so I began to pull myself over the other wounded and
I finally got to the deck. I could reach the railing of the other boat
and pulled myself onto it and lay there on the cabin deck as I was in
too much pain to pull myself any farther. Soon, one of the boys of my
regiment came to me. He was just a boy in his teens and small for his
age. He was wounded in the head but could walk all right. I had him
bunk with me. I saw a buffalo robe lying near me and in the after part
of the night I was in such pain from lying so long on my left side on
the hard floor, I had the boy spread the robe on the floor by my side
as I had seen noone [sic] was using the robe. I worked myself over to
the robe, but it was not long until a civilian gambler, who had gotten
himself appointed hospital steward for the trip in order to deadbeat
his passage up north, came and ordered me off the robe and
proceeded to curse me profusely. I asked him if the robe was his and
he answered by more cursing. I explained to him my condition and
told him that as I saw it was not in use I knew it would be a great
relief to my suffering, but that if it was his, of course, he could have it.
I talked gentlemanly to him but he came toward me and threatened
to kick me off if I did not get off instantly. This, I thought, was going
a little too far so I raised on my elbow, reached under my knapsack,
which I was using as a pillow, and in an instant he was enjoying the
very great pleasure of looking into the muzzle of my Navy. I gently
informed him that it was best for him to "git" and "git" fast or something would splash in the water below. It did not take him long to
catch the idea I was trying to convey to him, but when he got to the
cabin door he turned and said he would report me. I told him diplo-
matically to report and be damned. He soon returned and said, "The
general in command of the boat wishes to see you." I told him if the
general wished to see me he could come to me. He began cursing

again and ordered me off the robe. He had never yet claimed the robe as his so I again reached for my Navy and ordered him to leave and told him if he came near me again on the trip I would kill him as I would a viper. He never came near me anymore but I saw him kicking wounded soldiers and abusing them unmercifully, just because he knew they could not help themselves. I have always felt that I failed in my duty by not killing him, but am sure I would not have failed in that duty had I seen him kicking those wounded and helpless soldiers before he tried to abuse me.

Our boat started down the river Thursday morning, April 10th, and got to Paducah, Kentucky, Friday the 11th. There I got a piece of bread, which was the first food I had tasted since Sunday morning the 6th. We landed at Evansville, Ind., about midnight Friday night. I was then taken to a hospital. An 8th Missouri boy was one of the attendants in the hospital. The 8th Missouri and the 11th Indiana had always been brigaded together and were like brothers. He recognized me as of the 11th Indiana and had me placed on a cot right by the side of the door opening into the office of the surgeon who had charge of the hospital. As soon as this 8th Missouri soldier had the other wounded cared for, he came to me and asked if I would like a furlough home. I told him I would so he brought the surgeon out and he examined my wound, took my name, regiment and company and in a few minutes handed me a 30-day furlough home.[90]

The 8th Missouri boy took me in an ambulance to the depot and put me on the morning train. That evening I got to Ladoga, where my sister Cora was attending school. This was Saturday evening the 12th. The next morning my sister, with some friends took me home in a carriage. When we reached the old Hiland M.E. Church on our

---

[90] Actually Durham's furlough lasted more than thirty days, as he did not leave to rejoin his regiment until 26 May.

farm, the preacher had just started in on his sermon. I knew all my folks would be at the church and I called to a boy who was standing in front of the church and told him to go in and tell my father to come out. The boy recognized me and rushed into the church and made the announcement aloud, I suppose with some excitement. Suffice it to say, the meeting adjourned as quickly as if a fire had broken out. When I got home, my brother John, who was at home at that time, dressed my wound, which had not been dressed up to that time, I will not soon forget this dressing. My wound was fevered, the blood in the handkerchief was dried, caked and sticking tight to the flesh. It took my brother about two hours to get it loosened from the flesh.

Chapter 5

MEMPHIS AND HELENA

On May 26th I left home to join my regiment, took the train at Crawfordsville, went to New Albany, Indiana, and there I took a boat down the Ohio River to the mouth of the Tennessee River and up that river to Pittsburg Landing. I marched from the Landing to the regiment, which I reached on the 1st day of June near Corrinth [sic], Miss. The next day, June 2nd, General Wallace started with his division to march to Memphis, Tennessee. My wound was not yet healed up but I made the march all right. We reached Memphis on June 17th and camped there. In a few days we moved down the river to old Fort Hickman. This was near the Mississippi state line.[91]

One day while camped here I had charge of the picket line which was several miles southeast of the fort. My headquarters was on a public road in Mississippi just below the state line. About sunup one morning I saw an old negro coming up the road.[92] He was holding an old butcher knife in front of him, holding the blade in his hand with the handle pointing in front of him as a sign of surrender and friendship. The blade of the knife had been worn off until it was not two

---

[91] Durham actually meant Fort Pickering, a post garrisoned and extensively fortified by Union troops during the war, beginning in the summer of 1862 (US War Department, *The War of the Rebellion: A Compilation of the Official Records of the Union and Confederate Armies* [Washington, DC: Government Printing Office, 1880–1901] ser. 1, vol. 17, pt. 2, pp. 109, 259–62; ser. 1, vol. 49, pt. 2, pp. 899–901; US War Department, *Atlas to Accompany the Official Records of the Union and Confederate Armies* [Washington, DC: Government Printing Office, 1891–1895] 114).

[92] Durham was not the only Hoosier to come in contact with blacks in the region. A member of the regiment identified only as "H" wrote that along the line of march, whites would flee, hide in their houses or sit silently on their porches, but black residents would "come boldly out to meet us," answering questions and volunteering to carry water to the soldiers (Indianapolis *Daily Journal*, 20 June 1862).

inches long and he was naked except for the fragment of an old "breech-cloth" about four inches wide. His body or skin looked more like the hide of an alligator than of a human being. The large leaders in his legs had been cut just above the heels. The slave owners called this hamstringing, to keep them from running away. This old darky's body was one mass of scars from head to foot where he had been lacerated with whip and bloodhounds. He told me of the cruelties of his master; how his master had cut his flesh to pieces with the whip; how he had tried to run away to get away from these cruelties; how the bloodhounds caught him and tore his flesh so he came near dying; how, when he was caught and brought back to his master, his master hamstrung him, and how he finally escaped one night to a large swamp and by wading around in the water the hounds could not track him. He found a little island in the swamp and had lived alone for fourteen years. He would slip out at nights to a cornfield, get corn and with it coax hogs up to him and kill them with his old butcher knife. He had lived all these years on hogs and corn and had not seen a human being in all that time until the night before he came to me, when he saw a young negro who told him that there was a war going on and that the Yankies were freeing the negroes. The young negro told him where I was camped and he started at once to the Yankee line. He was the most pitiful sight I have ever seen. His skin was so calloused a mosquito could not penetrate it. I took him and turned him over to the provost marshall and never heard from him after that. I thought it would have been a good idea to have exhibited him to our copperheads in the North so they could see and have some conception of the curse of slavery.

Soon after we reached Memphis, General Lew Wallace was relieved of his command of our division and ordered to Cincinnati, Ohio. History gives his career after he left us.[93]

On July 24, 1862 we boarded a steamer and went down the Mississippi River to Helena, Arkansas and here we camped on the river bank. There was an Englishman in my company who had been a sailor. John C. Adkins and I were the best swimmers in the company.[94] Most all the boats going up and down the river had a yawl towed behind them and at night Adkins and I would swim out to the boats passing, cut the yawls loose from the boat, bring them ashore and the old sailor would rig them up with sails. It was not long until we had quite a number of these yawls. They were dubbed as "Company G's Fleet." We had much sport with our sailboats. I swam across the river where it was over three miles wide and had a yawl follow me so in case of accident it could come to my rescue. When I got tired swimming I would turn on my back and float until I got rested. I landed on the opposite side over a mile below where I started from.

I got a sergeant to get in a yawl with me one day to take a pleasure ride. I knew he could not swim and was cowardly and he knew I did not like him. When we got about the middle of the river I stopped the boat and told him I thought I would just upset the boat there and let him drown; that I could swim to shore and claim that it was an accident; that he had been acting the "pup" long enough and I had

---

[93] Wallace's reputation suffered as a result of his performance at Shiloh, and he did not receive a major command again until 1864. After being granted a leave of absence in June 1862, he ably prepared the city of Cincinnati against a threatened Confederate attack that fall, and helped organize Indiana troops to repel rebel General John Hunt Morgan's invasion of that state in the summer of 1863. In March 1864 he was given command of the Eighth Army Corps and the Middle Department (Delaware and part of Maryland). At the Battle of Monocacy MD in July 1864, Wallace was defeated by Confederate forces under General Jubal Early, but bought valuable time for the Federals to prepare for Early's assault on Washington two days later (Patricia L. Faust, ed., *Historical Times Illustrated Encyclopedia of the Civil War* [New York: Harper Collins Publishers, 1986] 504, 799).

[94] Adkins was a private from Montgomery County. He enlisted on 31 August 1861 and served until mustered out on 30 August 1864 (William H. H. Terrell, *Report of the Adjutant General of the State of Indiana*, vol. 4 [Indianapolis: Samuel M. Douglass, 1866] 189).

determined to get rid of him. It was great amusement to me to hear him beg for his life. He knew I could swim to shore very easily and knew I was aware of the fact that he could not swim a stroke or row a boat. The chump thought I was in dead earnest and knowing he had given me ample cause for disliking him, he felt sure his time had come. Finally, with seeming reluctance, I yielded to his pleadings and agreed to let him live a little while longer and see if there would be any improvement in his conduct. Had I been a Major General he could not have shown me more respect than he did after that "pleasure" boat ride.

On August 4th we started on a reconnoissance [sic] to Clarendon, Arkansas, a little town on White River. This town is about 65 miles west of Helena. This was one of our most disagreeable expeditions.[95] The weather was extremely hot and the enemy, in order to prevent us from getting any drinking water, had thrown dead carcasses in all the wells along the route of march. So our only chance for water was to get it out of the cypress swamps. The water in these swamps was covered with a green scum two inches thick, with the black viper or cotton mouth snakes (which are very poisonous) so thick in the water it looked as though they barely had room to wiggle. The water was as black as the strongest coffee; in addition to all its natural mixture of filth, our cavalry would ride their horses in the swamps, stirring the water and mud until it was more of a batter than a liquid, but we had to drink it or perish for water. Nearly the whole country from Helena to Clarendon was almost as level as a floor. The water in those cypress swamps was generally not over six inches deep and where there was no swamp the ground was covered with chap-

---

[95] On 4 August 1862, Brigadier General Alvin P. Hovey's division left Helena to "make a demonstration in the direction of Little Rock." On the evening of 7 August the division arrived in Clarendon AR between Helena and Little Rock, and remained there until 13 August. After sending out several expeditions from Clarendon and engaging in skirmishes with Confederate forces, Hovey returned to Helena on 17 August (*Official Records,* ser. 1, vol. 13, pp. 206–207).

arral bushes. These bushes are covered with thorns and matted together so it is impossible for a man to get through them except by crawling in trails made by wild animals.

We were greatly annoyed by bushwackers or guerrilla bands of the enemy. They would crawl in these trails and shoot from the brush where it was impossible to see them. Every soldier that gave out on the march and fell behind the command was killed from the brush by these guerrillas. I took sick on our return from Clarendon to Helena. I knew what my fate would be if I got behind the command so I marched until I fell by the side of the road. I was perfectly aware I would be killed as soon as the command passed me but I could go no further. But luck was on my side for once. Joe Hanna, a member of my company and who is now a brother-in-law, was driving a commissary wagon that day and he saw me along side of the road. He picked me up and dumped me in the wagon and hauled me to Helena, where I had a long spell of sickness. The surgeons did not seem to know what ailed me but finally decided that it was my spleen. All I know is that I suffered most fearfully from a pain in each side and it felt as though there was a knife blade about two inches wide plunged in each side. Every breath I drew this pain grew worse until I could hardly get breath enough to live on. I would not go to the hospital as they had nothing but a temporary affair and I did not like to hear others groaning around me. The surgeon finally ordered some of the men to get a stretcher and carry me to the hospital.

I was placed near a soldier whom I was satisfied was playing for a discharge from the army as he groaned and took on enough for a whole regiment in agony. I never could believe a fellow was very sick when he was extremely profuse with cries and loud groans. Whenever I could get breath enough in my lungs to speak, I used it all in abusing this fellow. Soon a preacher, with a face as long as a pump handle, came to me and asked me if I would not like to be at home where my mother could care for me. I gave him an angry look and in spite of my pain and short breath I told him if he had no more sense than to talk to a sick man in that way he should never go about the sick and that he ought to know it was hard for a sick man to keep from thinking and longing for home and that he knew I was not able to go home and nobody but a fool would try to turn a sick man's mind to home when he knew he could not go. I then ordered him to leave and not to come about me again.

That evening some of the boys of my company came to see me. I had them carry me back to my "downy" bunk. I will now try to give you an idea of this bunk. I had a fly tent over the bunk. A fly tent consists of four poles set in the ground in a square, about six feet high and then a square piece of canvas fastened to the top of the poles. This was my shelter. My bunk consisted of four forked sticks driven in the ground, two at the head and two at the foot. A stick was then laid in these forks, one at the head and the other at the foot. This made the head and foot rails and then poles laid lengthwise of the bunk and resting on these end pieces made the bed. I wish to testify on oath that the knots and limbs on these poles were not smoothed off very close. My bed consisted of one army blanket spread over these poles. I had to lie on this bunk for over two months and in all that time I was unable to find the soft side of those poles. While I was sick I was promoted from 4th Sergeant to First Orderly Sergeant.

November 16, 1862 we boarded a steamer and started down the Mississippi River to the mouth of White River where we had heard some of the enemy were encamped. We could not get up White River very far on account of low water. We had several skirmishes with the enemy but broke up their camps and dispersed them. We then dropped down the river twenty miles below the mouth of White River to Napolian [sic], Arkansas, where there were two regiments of the enemy camped. As it was a surprise to them when we landed and dashed down on their camp, they ran away with but little fighting. Bushwhackers fired on our boat a number of times from the river banks. We returned to Helena the 22nd.[96]

On the 27th of November we started on an expedition into the interior of Mississippi. We boarded a steamer and disembarked on the east side of the river several miles below Helena. We marched to the mouth of Cold Water River where it empties into the Tallahatchie River and here we encountered a body of cavalry and had a lively skirmish with them. Several were killed and wounded. Every day on this expedition we skirmished with the enemy. We returned to Helena December 7th.[97] On the 25th of December I was ordered on board the steamer Little Rocket with twenty-five men to guard a dispatch to General Sherman on the Yazoo River just above Vicksburg. I had a lively time on this trip. The bushwackers would fire on us from behind the levee every little while on our trip, both down and up the river. In some places they would open on us with an old cannon and when we got back the boat looked like an old tin lantern from having been punctured so often by bullets. Some of the boys got slight wounds but none serious. The water in the Yazoo

---

[96] Brigadier General Hovey determined to "make a dash" on the Confederate Post of Arkansas in November 1862. He embarked 8,000 men on steamers to go up the White River, but low water forced Hovey to turn back to Helena. Before doing so, he dispatched the 11th Indiana on the steamer *Rocket* to Napoleon AK to destroy a Confederate ferryboat. The Hoosiers accomplished the mission and returned. Hovey's report may be found in *Official Records*, ser. 1, vol. 13, pp. 358–60.

[97] In late November 1862, General Hovey launched an expedition from Helena AK to Delta MS with 5,000 infantrymen, 2,000 cavalrymen, and some artillery. He was to act in concert with General Ulysses S. Grant, who was moving into northern Mississippi. A Confederate army under Lieutenant General John C. Pemberton waited for Grant behind the Tallahatchie River, but Hovey's advance from the west threatened to outflank the rebels, and Pemberton's men withdrew from their strong position and retreated far to the south. Hovey's men crossed the Tallahatchie and on 1 December, skirmishers from the 11th Indiana fought with Confederate forces over the Yocknapatalfa River. After several hours of skirmishing the rebels withdrew. As Durham indicates, a few days later Hovey withdrew his forces back to Helena. His report of the expedition may be found in *Official Records*, ser. 1, vol. 17, pt. 1, pp. 530–32. A detailed account of this period may be found in Edwin Cole Bearss, *The Vicksburg Campaign*, vol. 1 (Dayton OH: Morningside House, 1985) 77–94. This three-volume study by Bearss, a former National Park Service chief historian, is considered the definitive work on the Vicksburg Campaign.

River was clear as a crystal and as we had been drinking the muddy water of the Mississippi River, when we saw the water in the Yazoo, we thought we would have water now that *is* water. We all went for it but only once, for it had a sweet brackish taste and ran through us like quick silver. We returned to Helena on December 31st.[98]

On January 11, 1863 nearly'all the troops encamped at Helena were put on board boats and sent down the Mississippi River and up White River to Davaulas [sic] Bluffs to act in conjunction with General Sherman in taking Arkansas Post which was located on the Arkansas River.[99] We disembarked at Davaulas Bluffs on the 17th and the snow was more than a foot deep and it was quite cold. It was said to be the deepest snow and coldest weather ever known there. Our regiment was sent out on picket duty that night, which meant no sleep but standing in snow knee-deep all night. As we could have no fire on the picket line, we suffered considerably from the cold. Deer tracks were as plentiful in the snow there as sheep tracks would be in a sheep pasture and we saw plenty of deer and could have killed them but dared not as a shot on the picket line would alarm the whole camp.

In the meantime General Sherman had captured Arkansas Post and on the 19th we embarked and started back to Helena.[100] Old General Gormand [sic] was in command of all the troops from Helena and we all disliked him.[101] At the mouth of the White River the boat carrying the General came alongside of ours and our boys

---

[98] At this time, Major General William T. Sherman was preparing to assault Chickasaw Bayou, just northeast of Vicksburg. His attack on 29 December 1862 was repulsed with heavy casualties. For a discussion of this operation, see Bearss, *Vicksburg Campaign*, vol. 1, 113–229.

[99] Actually Duvall's Bluff AK.

[100] Major General John A. McClernand was in command of the Arkansas Post expedition. He captured the fort and nearly 4,800 Confederates after a battle that lasted from 9–11 January 1863. Major General William T. Sherman led the 15th Army Corps in the operation (Bearss, *Vicksburg Campaign*, vol. 1, 405, 415–16).

began to "guy" his bodyguard. One of our fellows whom we called "Old Hoss" said something detrimental to the General and the General happened to hear his remark and ordered his guards to arrest Old Hoss, bring him aboard of his boat and tie him up by the thumbs to the flagstaff of the boat. The General kept him tied to the staff all night. When the boat landed at Helena Old Hoss was released and sent to his regiment and when he reached camp the boys began to laugh at him for being taken in by the old General but Old Hoss would not be downed, he replied with much contempt, "I don't want you common soldiers to talk to me, I have been serving on General Gormand's 'staff.'"[102]

We got back to Helena January 22d. In February 1863 the Mississippi River was higher than it had ever been known before. We crossed the river to the Mississippi side below Helena, cut the levee and let the water flow into the headwaters of the Yazoo River (see Grant's memoirs), with the object of carrying troops down the Yazoo River on transports and landing them where they could attack Vicksburg from the rear. This was an entertaining expedition. Our transports had to run through the woods and the limbs of the trees would rake the smokestacks and pilot houses off the boats and frequently raked soldiers off into the water, and the boats would often get fastened between trees. We had all kinds of trouble getting through this heavy timbered country with our boats. We thought our

---

[101] Willis Arnold Gorman (1816–1876), a Mexican War veteran, former congressman, and territorial governor of Minnesota, led the 1st Minnesota Infantry at the First Battle of Bull Run. Promoted to brigadier general, Gorman was placed in command of the District of Eastern Arkansas, and remained in the district even after he was replaced in February 1863. He was mustered out of the army in May 1864 (Ezra J. Warner, *Generals in Blue: Lives of the Union Commanders* [Baton Rouge: Louisiana State University Press, 1964] 178–79).

[102] General Gorman had already been unpopular with his men while serving as colonel of the 1st Minnesota Infantry and as a brigade commander in the Army of the Potomac from 1861 to late 1862. For examples, see Richard Moe's *The Last Full Measure: The Life and Death of the First Minnesota Volunteers* (New York: Henry Holt and Co., 1993) 65–68, 107, 136.

efforts were going to be crowned with success when we reached the junction of the Tallahatchie and Tallabusha Rivers which form the Yazoo proper. We were confident of smooth sailing soon as we reached the Yazoo but to our surprise we found a battery well fortified on an island in the river just below the junction of the two rivers named. As the whole country was overflowed by water there was no place we could place a battery to play on the enemy's battery, so we had to give up the expedition and return to Helena.[103]

There was nothing of much importance occurred in camp while we were encamped at Helena. Soon after we first went into camp there, the 12th Missouri, a German regiment, arrived and went into camp alongside of our camp. One day while most of our regiment was out on a scouting expedition, the 12th Missouri got on a drunk and raided our camp. Our boys, who were left in camp, fought them manfully, killing several of the 12th. After we returned to camp, the 12th renewed their attack, boasting they had "cleaned up" every regiment they had camped beside and proposed to clean us out. We did not think we needed cleaning out just at that time and when they came at us in an unorganized mass, we quickly formed our companies in regular line of battle with the intention of doing the thing up in strict accordance with army regulations. General McGinnis tried to quell their riot and a lieutenant tried to slash our adjutant general with his sword, but a little Mexican in our regiment was too quick for the lieutenant and busted his head with a club, killing him instantly. There would doubtless have been many of the 12th Missouri killed

---

[103] A reference to Ulysses S. Grant's Yazoo Pass Expedition. Grant's plan was to travel from Yazoo Pass, just below Helena on the Mississippi, into the Coldwater, Tallahatchie, and Yazoo Rivers, and finally arrive at Snyder's Bluff, just outside Vicksburg. The Federals managed to destroy a levee at the mouth of Yazoo Pass in early February 1863, and despite significant natural obstacles, were able to advance to Fort Pemberton, near Greenwood MS. There they were halted by a strong Confederate force. Repeated attempts to dislodge the rebels failed, and in early April the Federals withdrew. A detailed account of the expedition may be found in Bearss, *Vicksburg Campaign*, vol. 1, 479–548.

had not the general commanding the post arrived at this critical moment and ordered the 12th moved across the river on the Mississippi side in a camp all to themselves.[104]

Being Orderly Sergeant, it was my duty to form the company, making all details for duty, call the roll every morning at reveille and punish all who were not in ranks at roll call. About a mile back from the river at Helena there was a steep hill. When winter came, we moved our camp from the river bank to the foot of this hill. John R. Willey and Jake Buchanan, two members of my company, made a dugout in the side of the bluff.[105] They had a good door to their room and a chimney at the back end built from the fireplace up to a couple of feet above the surface of the hillside.[106] None of the boys liked "old Willey" as they called him, and at nights would pour "distilled water" down the chimney, or throw a dead dog or cat or most anything they could find, down the chimney; then Old Willey would rush out with his gun to shoot the perpetrators, only to find

---

[104] The incident began on the evening of 8 August 1862, when a member of Company E of the 11th Indiana fired his revolver from the riverbank into the river. The report startled a mule belonging to the 12th Missouri. One of the Missourians then used a stick of wood to knock the offending Hoosier into the river. The Missourian then strutted through Company E's camp uttering threats, and was "fearfully punished." This action brought reinforcements from both sides, and after clubs, bottles, and brickbats were thrown, some of the Hoosier officers managed to restore order. Several men on both sides were seriously injured. A member of the 11th described the incident as a "disgraceful and shameful" occurrence. Despite Durham's claims, no member of the 12th Missouri was killed in the melee (*Indianapolis Daily Journal*, 19 August 1862; personal correspondence with Dr. Earl J. Hess, Harrogate, Tennessee, 23 January 2000).

[105] Privates Jacob Buchanan and John R. Willey of Montgomery County both enlisted in Company G, 11th Indiana, on 31 August 1861. Buchanan later became a second lieutenant in the 1st Regiment Arkansas Volunteers, African Descent (46th United States Colored Infantry), and resigned on 9 October 1863. Willey was discharged from the 11th Indiana on 31 January 1864, due to disability (Terrell, *Report of the Adjutant General*, vol. 4, 189–90; US Adjutant General's Office, *Official Army Register of the Volunteer Force of the United States Army*, vol. 8 [Washington, DC: Adjutant General's Office, 1865] 219).

[106] The members of the 11th Indiana started to build winter quarters as early as mid-October. One soldier reported the "busy hum of industry" (hut construction) around camp, with sounds similar to those heard in "some large manufacturing depot." The men used lumber confiscated from local cotton gins to erect "chibangs" and form "a thriving country village" (*Indianapolis Daily Journal*, 31 October 1862).

they had already "shot" to a hiding place. After they built this dugout, Willey and Buchanan often failed to be at roll call in the morning and I would punish Buchanan by making him march up and down the company quarters with a fence rail or pole on his shoulder. He was a neighbor boy at home and as soon as I would relieve him at night he would come to my tent and talk over old times at home as though nothing had happened. I have never known anyone to take punishment so good naturedly as he did. But it was different with old Willey, as he was the most contrary and ill-grained man I have ever seen, and at the same time a rank coward. He could smell a battle from afar and would always take the "dry-grypes" before the battle opened up so he would not be able to go into battle; in fact, I never did succeed in getting him into battle, but after the battle was over he was the first one to go to the other regiments and blow about what "we did."

Old Willey finally refused to attend roll call so I sent a corporal with a couple of the boys to arrest him and bring him to me. He had his door barred and refused to open the door and told them he would shoot them if they tried to get in. They told him they would report him to the orderly and he informed them that if I came near his shack he would kill me. As soon as they reported this to me, I went and kicked his door in. He was standing inside with his gun cocked but I sprang in quick as the door went in, grabbed his gun and downed him before he realized what was happening. I took him to company quarters, bucked and gagged him and put a couple of the boys to guard him whom I knew he despised. But this was not enough for the old pup (I call him old because he was the oldest man in the company for he must have been nearly fifty years old). When he refused to attend roll call next morning and sent me word he would make a hole in my vest if I tried to arrest him again, I took him and tied him up by the thumbs. This brought the old whelp to time

[sic] but he never forgave me. He was the only soldier I ever had to buck and gag or tie up by the thumbs. With the exception of this old fellow, I seldom ever had to punish any of the men, not even with extra duty. They all liked me and took pride in obeying orders.

As some of my readers may not know what "buck and gag" means, I will explain. A soldier is set flat on the ground, his hands tied together, then his knees are raised, his feet brought back near his seat, his hands slipped over his knees and a stick is run through under his knees, and then a stick or cloth is put in his mouth and fastened around the back of his head. This looks like cruelty but it is an established mode of punishment in the army when no milder punishment will subdue a rebellious soldier. It often requires severe punishment to maintain discipline in the army.

Chapter 6

VICKSBURG

The morning of April 12, 1863, we boarded a steamer and started down the Mississippi River to Vicksburg. We got to Millikins Bend the night of the 13th. The 14th we disembarked and pitched tents. It was raining all the time and the mud was knee deep. The 15th we remained in camp and on the 16th we started on a march to Carthage, Louisiana.[107] Here we left our knapsacks, tents and everything except an oilcloth blanket, haversack and canteen. We did not see our tents and knapsacks, which contained all our earthly possessions, until late in June while beseiging Vicksburg. On the 18th we bivouacked on Dawson's plantation. We remained here until the 21st, building bridges across bayous, etc. On the 20th of April I was promoted to 2nd Lieutenant of my Company G. I knew nothing of this promotion until it was read out in dress parade. I should have stated that on the 19th the regiment presented General George F. McGinnis with a sword and sash, horse saddle and accoutrements, in honor of his promotion to Brigadier General. This same morning I went to our quartermaster John W. Coons, a dutchman, to draw rations for the company.[108] I had run out of the blanks we generally

---

[107] Actually the village of New Carthage, about 35 miles downstream from Vicksburg (Edwin Cole Bearss, *The Vicksburg Campaign*, vol. 2 [Dayton OH: Morningside House, 1985] 24–25).

[108] John W. Coons of Indianapolis was formally commissioned and mustered as quartermaster of the 11th Indiana in June 1863, but must have been serving as acting quartermaster as early as April. He was mustered out in December 1864. Prior to this appointment he served as a second lieutenant in Durham's own Company G, and his promotion to quartermaster allowed Durham to receive a commission (William H. H. Terrell, *Report of the Adjutant General of the State of Indiana*, vol. 2 [Indianapolis: W. R. Holloway, 1865] 76, 81).

used in making out our requisitions. The quartermaster had always furnished the orderly sergeants with these blanks for his own convenience, though I had filled out so many requisitions for the company I knew the form as well as I did my ABCs. I wrote my requisition on a blank paper and handed it to him and he dashed it back at me, and, holding up a blank, said, "This is the kind of a thing to make a requisition on," and in order to show off before some officers of other commands who were present, proceeded to give me a cussing. I knew the requisition was in perfect form, he knew it and knew I had been making requisitions for the company for nearly two years and knew the form as well as he did. I asked him what was wrong with the requisition and he said there was not paper enough. I told him if he would furnish me with a blank I would make one out on it, so he said, "Damn you, furnish your own paper." When I turned to leave an officer whom I had never seen before and who had been listening to the quartermaster's abuse, called to me and said "Here Orderly, I have plenty of paper," and handed me a sheet of foolscap paper. I wrote my requisition on this paper as fine and close together as I could and took it and handed it to the quartermaster, saying, "If this is not paper enough to suit you, I can get more[."] He not only saw his spread-eagle display did not take well with the officers present, but saw I was not feeling real pleasant about it, he said, "Oh damn it, there is no use getting mad about it." I then told him I knew his position and knew mine and that if we were equal in rank it would be settled very differently. I said, "You will please just make a note of this, for the time will come when I will settle it more satisfactorily to myself." It was next to high treason for a private or non-commissioned officer to strike a commissioned officer. I knew this tied my hands but it so happened that the very next day I was promoted to Lieutenant, which placed me on equal footing with him. It is unnecessary to say that from that day I was on the lookout for an excuse to dress his head up so it would be presentable in fairly good society.

On the 21st we left Dawson plantation. Our object was to reach the river below Vicksburg. On the 22d we reached Dunbar's plantation and bivouacked in the negro quarters. Here we were delayed three days building a bridge across another bayou. On Saturday night, the 25th, our transports ran the blockade at Vicksburg. There was heavy cannoning for three days and only one transport was sunk.[109] On the 27th, having finished our bridge, we continued our march. It rained hard all day and the mud was knee deep. We bivouacked for the night within two miles of the river. On the 28th we reached the river above Grand Gulf and here we found our transports that had run the blockade at Vicksburg. We bivouacked on the river bank and that night about midnight, General John A. Logan called the generals into council of war and asked them if any of them had a regiment that could be trusted to hold the ground if landed in front of the forts at Grand Gulf until reinforcements could be landed. General A.P. Hovey, our division commander, said "Yes, I have the Eleventh Indiana in my division and if you ordered them to storm Hell they would do it and nine chances out of ten they would take it." Logan then said, "That is the regiment I want." General Logan then sent for all the officers of the regiment and then gave us our orders, viz. "You are to board at once the steamer Forest Queen. Be in readiness to steam across the river the moment our gunboats silence the batteries on the forts. The moment the barge which is attached to the Forest Queen strikes the opposite bank, you are to spring across the barge and onto the bank and hold your position until the boat returns to this side and takes reinforcements to you. Any officer or

---

[109] Durham was slightly in error about this date. The six transports ran past Vicksburg on the night of 22 April, losing one ship (Bearss, *Vicksburg Campaign*, vol. 2, 75–79).

soldier who flinches from duty you are to shoot down on the spot. You are to hold this position as long as there is a man left alive." This was about two o'clock in the morning and I must confess when General Logan had explained the situation and desperateness of the case and gave us such binding orders, my knees felt just a little shaky.[110] About three o'clock we were aboard the boat and about daylight we dropped down the river just out of range of the guns in the fort. Our troops were on the west side of the river and the fort on the east side. Grand Gulf was located on the lower side of the mouth of Black River where it empties into the Mississippi River.

This morning of April 29th about eight o'clock, our gunboat fleet opened fire on the forts and continued the bombardment until after one o'clock p.m. This battle between our fleet and the rebel forts at Grand Gulf was the grandest sight I have ever witnessed. From our position on the Forest Queen, we had a fine view of the forts and our fleet. I could see the effect of the shots from either side. Our fleet consisted of eight gunboats. The battle was most terrific and lasted five hours and a half. The fort was on a high bluff and our gunboats failed to silence a single gun of the enemy so far as we could see. Our fleet lost about twenty killed and sixty wounded. The majority of the killed and wounded were on the flag boat where a shell penetrated the side of the boat and exploded between the decks where our men were working their guns. All during this battle, General Grant was on a little tug boat called "Little Corporal" and he was right among the

---

[110] The meeting with General Logan that Durham describes cannot be found in other accounts. It seems highly unlikely that Logan, a division commander in the 17th Army Corps, would ask for a regiment from General John McClernand's 13th Corps. On the other hand, a meeting between General Hovey and his brigade and regimental commanders did take place in the wardroom of the *Forest Queen* about midnight on 28 April. It is quite possible that this is the meeting Durham is referring to, and perhaps General George McGinnis offered the 11th to General Hovey, instead of Hovey offering the regiment to Logan (Bearss, *Vicksburg Campaign*, vol. 2, 297; Theodore T. Scribner, *Indiana's Roll of Honor* [Indianapolis: A. D. Streight, 1866] 266).

gunboats, running from one to another. I felt very uneasy for his safety.[111]

We remained on our boat in the river until after dark, when we marched on the levee below Grand Gulf. We could not easily have gotten below Grand Gulf had it not been for the levee, for the whole country back of the levee was covered with water. Nor could we have used the levee in daytime as it would have been in plain sight of the enemy. Our fleet and transports ran the blockade that night and on the morning of April 30th the enemy found out our fleet and all our troops were below Grand Gulf. Grant had expected to go to Rodney to cross the river, which was 9 miles below Grand Gulf, but in the night an old colored man informed Grant of a crossing at Bruinsburg a few miles above Rodney. From this point a road ran to Port Gibson, some 12 miles in the interior. We got across to the east side of the river on the 30th. The transports and gunboats were used in placing us across. The boats had to make several trips in crossing all the troops as we had about 20,000 in all. We marched in the direction of Port Gibson as soon as we were landed across the river. About two miles out from the river was high ground and Grant was anxious to get possession of this high ground before meeting the enemy. Bayou Pierre ran through Port Gibson and lay between our army and Grand Gulf and the only bridge across this bayou was located at Port Gibson. Grant knew that the enemy at Grand Gulf would have to go to Port Gibson to cross the bayou and therefore he was anxious to get to Port Gibson before the enemy could reach there, in order to get

---

[111] Durham is largely correct in his account of the fighting at Grand Gulf. The Federal naval bombardment began at 7:50 A.M. and continued until 1:15 P.M., when Union forces broke off the action. Eight Union ships were involved in the operation and suffered a total of eighteen killed and fifty-seven wounded. USS Tuscumbia suffered the largest number of casualties due to Confederate shells piercing her armor and bursting inside the ship. Durham is incorrect in two details, however. General Grant was on board the ship Ivy, not Little Corporal, and in fact the fire of the Federal warships did manage to dismount two Confederate 32-pounder guns (Bearss, Vicksburg Campaign, vol. 2, 309–15).

possession of the bridge before it could be destroyed by the enemy. But before daylight we met the rebel General Bowen with eight or ten thousand troops within four miles west of Port Gibson.[112] This night march out from the river in a country we had no knowledge of whatever and expecting to run onto the enemy every moment, was rather impressive. We muffled the wheels of our artillery and commands were given but little louder than a whisper. As this was our third night without sleep many of the men were asleep while marching. The instant a halt was made the men would drop in the road asleep. I remember one incident that night. We were marching up a hill. We halted. The men were asleep as soon as they dropped to the ground. Soon a racket broke loose on top of the hill ahead of us. It sounded like a cavalry charge and this startled our sleeping soldiers and from impulse, not reason, they all sprang out of the road to avoid being run over in the supposed charge. As there were deep gullies on either side of the road, several were injured but none seriously. I, like the rest, sprang to my feet but when I came to my senses I found myself alone in the road with my sword drawn and squared for defense. I have found this a queer part of my nature. When I am badly startled and act wholly from impulse, I never scream or start to run as most people do, but when I come to my reason I always find myself standing in the spot where I was startled and ready for defense. I have never known what this racket was that startled us so.

Before daylight we met the enemy at the old Magnolia Church. There was a little skirmishing before day, but soon after daylight we got down to business. This was the first day of May 1863. I thought it

---

[112] On 30 April 1863, Grant's 13th and 17th Army Corps were ferried across the Mississippi River to the eastern shore and began to march on Vicksburg. At Port Gibson, about ten miles from the river, Brigadier General John S. Bowen of Missouri and about 7,000 Confederates bravely faced the approaching 24,000 Federals. The battle began early on the morning of 1 May 1863, and Bowen's troops fought until early that evening before being forced to retreat (Bearss, *Vicksburg Campaign*, vol. 2, 402–407).

a shame to fight there, right at the church.[113] It was a beautiful and pleasant morning and we were in a forest of magnolia trees which were in full bloom. The beauty of the large blooms and their fragrance made me feel more like admiring the beauties of nature than fighting. We drove the enemy back to the main body of their troops, skirmishing all the while. The 34th Indiana, which was to our right in the line of battle, ran on to the main body of the enemy first. They started to charge a battery; it got too hot for them and they dropped to the ground and were lying flat in an old field, unable to go either forward or backward without great loss of life. The enemy were facing west and we were facing east. The rebel battery was located just south of an old log cabin. One gun was at the southeast corner of the cabin. There was a lane running from the cabin west to the road and the road ran north and south. North of the lane from the cabin was a woods pasture. South of the lane was an old field. The road ran along the west fence of the field and pasture. When our regiment came up to the support of the 34th Indiana, we found them about fifty yards inside of the field lying flat on the ground and some were in the lane. When we halted in the road my company was right across the mouth of the lane. We were ordered to lie down as the rebel battery was throwing grape and canister down the lane and tearing up the earth. I said to my company, "Boys, I had just as leave die going toward that thing as to die here—let's go take it." They said all right. I then sprang to my feet, waved my sword and gave a yelp and we dashed up the lane at the battery with all the speed there was in us. When we reached the yard fence we jumped it clear and then

---

[113] The Battle of Port Gibson was fought simultaneously in two different areas. While Federal forces on the left flank under Brigadier General Peter J. Osterhaus battled along the Bruinsburg Road, Durham and his comrades in the 11th Indiana on the Federal right fought on the Rodney Road, led by corps commander Major General John A. McClernand. For a detailed account of Port Gibson, see Bearss, *Vicksburg Campaign,* vol. 2, 353–407.

turned to the left so as to throw the cabin between us and the battery. About half the company went to the right and the others to the left of the cabin. I went to the right and then rounding the southwest corner we found ourselves facing the mouth of a cannon not over 15 feet in front of us, loaded to the muzzle with grape and canister—with the gunner "lanyard" in hand and in the act of firing it. I yelled "Boys, shoot the gunner." I hardly had the words spoken when there must have been twenty bullets put through his body. I thought when the boys fired, 'now if his muscles should contract as is generally the case when one is killed instantly, he will clinch the lanyard and fire the gun as he falls.' But instead his hands flew open wide and with both hands above his head he sprang high from the ground and dropped dead. I do not think I ever saw a man jump so high as he did.

° Under such excitement and high pressure as we were under, when we rounded the corner of the cabin almost in the mouth of that cannon, it is astonishing how fast and quick one can think and act. The whole thing was transacted in the twinkling of an eye. A delay of one second in shooting the gunner would have resulted in the destruction of myself and half of my company. The moment the gunner was killed I ordered the boys to shoot the artillery horses so the other cannons and caisons [sic] could not be hauled off the field. We either killed or drove the artillery men from their guns, turned the cannon we had captured by the cabin, and fired its load of grape and canister into the infantry that were supporting the battery. We had passed beyond the battery and were in hot combat with, and driving the enemy before us, when the 34th Indiana and some from other regiments came up. Their officers jumped astride the guns and claimed their capture, while at the same time my company was between them and the enemy, driving them back and taking pris-oners. I thought at the time it showed quite an enlarged cheek for them to claim the capture after we had shot the horses and had driven the enemy from the guns and was at that time between them and the enemy. They were so elated at the capture that they halted at the guns and held them while we were fighting against odds of at least ten to one. Of course, I would have been done for had the remainder of my regiment not come to my assistance. We captured about three hundred prisoners.[114]

In the charge on this battery my sword scabbard was torn from my belt so I could not sheathe my sword. Among the prisoners we took was a rebel captain. He surrendered his sword to me and as he was about my size, I threw my sword down and buckled his on, and I carried that sword during the remainder of my service and it now adorns a wall in the house of my nephew and namesake.

In this charge and battle I did not lose a man but several were wounded. We captured the guns, drove the enemy off the field and captured about three hundred soldiers. The secret of my success was in the boldness of the dash. It seemed to fluster the enemy and we had them going before they realized that there were not a million of us. I received no open credit for capturing this battery. My name was not even mentioned in any of the reports of the battle. This battle was known, and is known in history, as the Battle of Port Gibson. The nearest mention of my capture of this battery that I have found in any of the reports of the battle, was in the report of General A.P. Hovey, who commanded our division. He said, "Just before I ordered a charge I heard yelling, looked and saw what I took to be [a] company of the 11th Indiana at the guns. I knew they were the 11th

---

[114] Durham is essentially in agreement with other participants regarding this part of the action. Brigade commander General Alvin P. Hovey did order the 34th Indiana forward to capture the Confederate artillery pieces, but the Hoosiers were stopped by heavy enemy fire. Shortly afterward he directed the center of the Union line to charge, and the Federals captured 2 howitzers from the Botetourt Virginia Artillery, along with 3 caissons and more than 200 prisoners. Although considerable controversy exists as to which regiment captured the cannons, as Durham explains later in the narrative, his claim that the 11th Indiana deserves the honor is as valid as any other (Bearss, *Vicksburg Campaign,* vol. 2, 379–81).

Indiana from their uniforms." When Colonel Cameron of the 34th Indiana claimed the capture of the guns in his report to General McGinnis, the General at first refused to accept the report, saying, "I saw who captured that battery."[115] Then Colonel Cameron and colonels of other regiments all claiming the capture, joined in a great furor against General McGinnis, claiming he was partial to his old regiment and wanted to give them all the credit. As he saw it was going to create enmity and prejudice against him by the colonels under him, he let them all make their reports to suit themselves; but the main reason he did not refuse these reports, which he knew were not correct, was that I made the charge without orders. This subjected me to courtmartial and dismissal from the service and had he contended for my rights he knew they would prefer charges against me for violating military regulations. Had I been unsuccessful I would doubtless have been courtmartialed.

General McGinnis himself could not say much for when we started on the charge the general was up the lane fence a short distance and as we dashed by he sprang up to his feet, waived his sword and yelled, "Go in my boys, you have never failed me yet and I know you won't now." When I first saw him wave his sword I thought he was motioning us back but we were under such headway there was no turning back then. I was greatly relieved when I heard him shout, "go in my boys." I did not think of claiming any honors. I thought I was simply doing my duty. But I think General McGinnis felt there were honors due me that I had not received, for a short time after this he came to me and told me he could get me a commission as colonel

---

[115] Robert Alexander Cameron (1828–1894), a newspaper publisher and Indiana politician, first joined the 9th Indiana (three months), then became colonel of the 34th Indiana Infantry. He led that regiment at the capture of Island No. 10 and the siege of Vicksburg. Appointed a brigadier general of volunteers, Cameron commanded a division in the Red River Campaign and ended the war a brevet major general (Ezra J. Warner, *Generals in Blue: Lives of the Union Commanders* [Baton Rouge: Louisiana State University Press, 1964] 64–65).

of a regiment if I would accept it, as I had won the promotion at Port Gibson. But owing to my limited education at the time I refused to accept the honor. I knew I could drill and handle the men and maneuver and command them in battle as well and far better than many colonels I had seen, but a colonel has the responsibility for all the arms and supplies of the regiment and that required much clerical work which I did not feel capable of doing and my pride never allowed me to accept any position I could not fill equal to the best. But I can now see where I was foolish and if it were possible to do it over again I would accept the honor and would get an educated man for adjutant and let him do the clerical work.

There was a dispute carried on in articles written for the National Tribune, a soldier paper, published at Washington, D.C., by members of those different regiments who claimed the capture of this battery at Port Gibson, Mississippi, for at least twenty-five years after the war, and it seemed to never have been settled satisfactorily to anyone and I suppose it will go down in history as an unanswered question.[116] I have never written an article making any claim to the capture, due to the fact that I feared some would claim I was trying to manufacture a great big "I."

I remember very distinctly looking back after we had passed the battery and were fighting the infantry that was supporting the battery, and seeing a lieutenant whom I took to be of the 34th Indiana regiment, jump astride the gun we had just turned on the enemy and fired with our own hands. It amused me to see him jump off so much quicker than he jumped on and the way he rubbed his

---

[116] The *National Tribune* began publication in 1877 as a newspaper for Union veterans. Intended to inform veterans about pension issues, the paper also included reminiscences about battles and soldier life. In 1926 it became known as the *National Tribune Stars and Stripes*, and gradually ended its Civil War coverage as those veterans died. For a discussion of the Battle of Port Gibson and the capture of the Confederate guns, see "Still Another-The 11th Ind." by 11th Indiana veteran John R. Holbrook in the 4 December 1884 issue.

sitting-down place with his hand, I took it for granted the gun was still hot. A soldier by the name of Halbrook, who was a gunner in General Price's army and who had deserted the rebel army and had enlisted with us, fired the gun.[117]

Several amusing things occurred in this battle. John I. Cook of my company was at my side when he shot a rebel in front of us. He slapped his hand on his thigh and said, "By G—, Pap Durham, did you see me turn that d—d rebel's belly to the sun?" The head of a ravine ran back of the battery we took and there was a large log lying across the head of this ravine. Many of the enemy had jumped over this log and down into the ravine to shield themselves from our bullets. Joseph Hanna, a member of my company, was about 20 feet from this log with his gun cocked and his finger on the trigger, ready to shoot in an instant, when a rebel sprang upon the log, threw his gun down on Hanna, saying, "You d—d Yankee, I will get you now." Hanna, quicker than a flash, threw his gun out without taking aim and fired and the rebel fell off back of the log dead. [118] Then Hanna, who talked very slow, said, after he had shot, "You d—d rebel, you had better be in a hurry about it." I was impressed right there that it sometimes makes quite a difference in cussing before or cussing afterward. Ever since this incident I have thought it the best policy if a fellow had to cuss at all it was best act first, then do the cussing act.

After the enemy had retreated we followed them up to where they made another stand on a ridge. Our troops were in a valley and a swampy creek ran through the valley. This valley was covered with timber and underbrush. Beyond this strip of swamp and timber there

---

[117] Possibly John R. Holbrook, a member of Company E, 11th Indiana, and a resident of Rondo, Conway County AK in 1884 (*National Tribune*, 4 December 1884).

[118] Privates Cook and Joseph T. Hanna, both residents of Montgomery County, enlisted in Company G on 31 August 1861, and were mustered out on 30 August 1864 (Terrell, *Report of the Adjutant General*, [Indianapolis: Samual M. Douglass, 1866] vol. 4, 189).

was an old field that extended up to the ridge where the enemy made their stand. As we had no cavalry across the river as yet, my company was sent out on the right as lookouts to protect our right flank. We went to the right of our right flank and out in front, in the direction of the enemy. We took our station on a high knoll where we could see in all directions. About the time we reached this knoll, General Bowen, who was in command of the rebel troops, made a charge on our line.

We were in position to see the whole charge and the fighting without taking part in it. I must say a battle is a grand sight where a fellow can stand off and look at it. Our troops repulsed the charge. We had great sport when the enemy began to straggle back across the field to the ridge where they started from. We would shoot close to them and demand their surrender. Most of them would turn and come to us and surrender on the first shot but some would not stop when we demanded their surrender and we would shoot close to them, making the dirt fly up around them and they would finally round in and surrender. I do not remember of us having to kill any of them for it was not our desire to kill them unless they refused to surrender. In the hope of getting our favor, most all of them claimed they were forced into the army, but one red-whiskered, red-headed Missourian, whom we thought we would have to "wing" before he would surrender, swore he had fought as long as he had any ammunition and would be fighting yet if he had had the ammunition. We rather liked his grit. This repulse of Bowen's charge ended the battle of Port Gibson. We had driven the enemy back several miles and we were now within about two miles of Port Gibson.[119]

---

[119] Losses in the 11th Indiana were surprisingly light. The regiment suffered only one man killed, twenty-three wounded, and one missing (Bearss, *Vicksburg Campaign,* vol. 2, 403).

We bivouacked for the night and started for Port Gibson before daylight the morning of May 2nd. On reaching Port Gibson, we found the enemy had burned the bridge across the bayou so we at once went to work constructing a bridge. This was a kind of raft bridge. We tore down old stables and fences for material for the bridge and we got the bridge finished by evening. Port Gibson was a beautiful little town. It had a girl's college there but the school was dismissed in our honor and the girls dispersed. We found many wounded rebel soldiers there from the battle of the day before.

On Sunday morning, May 3d, we crossed the bayou on our bridge and moved in the direction of Vicksburg and bivouacked at Willow Springs some ten miles from Port Gibson. We were driving the enemy all day, which meant a constant skirmish. We remained all day the 4th at Willow Springs, waiting for our ammunition train. Learning here that Grand Gulf was evacuated by the enemy, I was ordered to take command of a detail of one hundred men and take our prisoners (about 600 in number) to Grand Gulf. I started with the prisoners early the morning of the 5th. We reached Grand Gulf late that afternoon. I was also ordered to bring back with me the horses of the field officers which had been left on the west side of the Mississippi River. I could not get a boat to take me across the river that night so I spent the night on the steamer Empire City. In the meantime I had turned my prisoners over to the provost marshall.

On the afternoon of the 6th, I crossed the river on the Forest Queen, got the horses on board and stayed there until nearly dark when General W.T. Sherman came up with the advance of his corps.[120] He stood by the gang plank, hurrying his men up. The first regiment to be put on board was our old "friends" the 12th Missouri.

[120] General William T. Sherman's Fifteenth Army Corps began crossing the Mississippi to join the rest of Grant's army on the night of 6 May, and the task was completed the following night (Bearss, *Vicksburg Campaign*, vol. 2, 451). The 12th Missouri was part of the Second Brigade, 1st Division of that corps.

I could soon see and hear them saying to each other, "There is one of them d—d 11th Indiana fellows," and they all began to look very fierce at me. I felt a little ticklish as I did not feel absolutely certain that I was good for a whole regiment. In the meantime some of them got to grumbling about being too crowded. General Sherman heard them and he turned loose with the most profane profanity I ever heard. He ordered his orderly to bring another regiment on the double quick and to one of his aide-de-camps to bring another. Then he turned to the 12th Missouri and said, "Damn you, I will teach you what it is to kick about being crowded." He put two more regiments on the boat and we were all standing up and were packed in as tight as sardines in a box. All this time Sherman was standing by the gang plank, making the air blue with his cursing the men for not moving faster. As a "cusser" he was the finest artist at the business that you could imagine. The old boat was loaded down so the water was slopping over the deck. I expected to see her go down every minute. We got across that night by 2 o'clock and got my horses off the boat. I spent the remainder of the night on the steamer Anglo Saxon.

While at Grand Gulf I examined the rebel forts and found them the most impregnable works I had ever seen. I felt more than glad that our fleet could not silence their guns for we would have had to land in front of the forts. The forts were located on a high bluff fronting the river. Between the river and bluff there was a strip of level ground about one-quarter of a mile wide right at the base of this bluff. There were rifle pits one above another from the base of this bluff to the top, with trenches or tunnels cut from one line of rifle pits to the other; so if we should drive the enemy out of the lower pits they could fall back into the next pit above without being exposed and could keep this process up to the top of the bluff. One man in these trenches or rifle pits would have been equal to a half dozen men outside. Had we landed in front of this bluff as was intended in case the guns in the forts were silenced, the men in these trenches would have mowed us down faster than we could possibly have landed troops. I saw it was very fortunate for us that the guns in the fort were not silenced. On the morning of the 7th I started back to my regiment.

I got within seven miles of the regiment that night and bivouacked for the night. I reached the regiment in the forenoon of the 8th and found them in line of battle. We drove the enemy to within two miles of the Big Black River.

We kept up a lively skirmish here for two days and sometimes it would almost reach the dignity of a regular battle. We were receiving small reinforcements all the time. This was what is called a "feint." Our object was to get the enemy to concentrate his force there, thinking that was the point where we intended to make our main attack. The enemy bit at the bait and concentrated their whole army there—that is, the army under General Pemberton. While we were holding the enemy here the main bulk of our army was making a forced march to Jackson, the capitol of Mississippi, for the purpose of driving General Joe Johnson [sic] out of Jackson, capturing the city and destroying the supplies and manufacturing establishments. On the 10th we marched in the direction of Jackson so as to be in reach in case we were needed there. We passed through and bivouacked three miles beyond Cayuga, Miss. On the morning of the 12th we moved in the direction of Edwards Station and had heavy skirmishing all day. We drove the enemy across Fourteen Mile Creek and bivouacked for the night on the creek bank. On the 13th we drove the enemy to within two miles of Edwards Station, leading them to believe we were intending to make our main attack there and after a heavy skirmish and great show of a general attack, we turned and marched rapidly in the direction of Jackson by way of Raymond.

General Logan and General McPherson had a fight with the enemy at Raymond where they were met by five thousand of the enemy with two batteries of field artillery under command of General Greeg [Gregg]. Our loss was sixty-six killed, three hundred and thirty-nine wounded and thirty-seven missing. The enemy's loss was one hundred killed, three hundred and five wounded, besides we took four hundred and fifteen prisoners. We bivouacked for the night at Seven Mile Creek.

On the 14th we marched through Raymond and in the direction of Clinton, which is eight miles from Jackson and on the Jackson and Vick[s]burg railroad. It rained in torrents all the night of the 13th and until 10:00 a.m. on the 14th. The roads were almost impassable and some places the water was more than a foot deep on the ground, but we were between two armies of the enemy. On our left was General Pemberton with fifty thousand men for the defense of Vicksburg and on our right was General Joseph E. Johnson [sic] with an army of twelve thousand men at Jackson, the capitol of the State, with reinforcements coming in all the time. Pemberton's army around Vicksburg was nearly twice the size of our army and a few days delay and Johnson's [sic] army would have been as large or larger than our own. General Grant's plan was by rapid movement to force himself in between these two armies and fight them in detail. Therefore, rain or no rain, roads or no roads, hungry or thirsty, we had to move rapidly. Very little time was taken for sleep and we were on the move almost constantly both day and most of the night. Nor had we had any rations for two weeks. Our bill of fare was mostly parched corn and we used it for food and coffee. But the soldiers did not grumble. In the first place they liked Grant and had all all [sic] confidence in his generalship and were anxious for his sake to see his efforts crowned with victory. Each soldier had a burning desire for this campaign to be a success as the rebels had so loudly boasted that we could never take Vicksburg and, furthermore, we all knew well the situation and fully appreciated the fact that for us it was victory or destruction. Therefore, we were all determined that it should be victory and were willing to undergo any hardships and privations to that end.

On the 14th, General Sherman and General McPherson captured Jackson and drove General Joseph E. Johnson [sic] out of the city. As I did not take part in this first capture of Jackson, my readers can get the facts from history or Grant's Memoirs. On the 15th we marched to Clinton and there we turned west on the main Vicksburg and Jackson road and moved in the direction of Vicksburg. We bivouacked for the night within one mile of Bolton Depot. On May 16th we moved early in the morning in the direction of Edwards Station. We had only marched three miles when we came upon the enemy in full force. It was Pemberton's whole army we were facing. Every soldier knew that the question as to the success or failure of our campaign was to be settled there and then. We knew the enemy was far superior to us in numbers, and we knew our defeat meant the practical destruction of our army. Therefore, everyone was determined to make a desperate fight. In a case like this the intelligence of the common soldier counts for much. It is almost impossible to whip an army where the common soldier, or rank and file of the army, is unable to grasp the situation or know what they have to do to gain the victory. The enemy had taken position on Champions [sic] Hill, which overlooked the whole country around. It was a fine strategic position, the best that could have been found in that country. The first knowledge I had that the enemy was close in our front in great numbers was just before we came onto their pickets. There was an old fat, bench-legged negro aunty standing in a fence corner by the side of the road. As we passed by I asked her a joshing question. She did not understand my question but answered, "Yes, sah—yes, sah, dars just thousands of them, thousands of 'em just on ahead dar." As the boys near me heard the question I asked her and heard her answer, they raised a yell that was taken up by the troops and carried for miles back along the line. When we got to Champion's house, which stood near the road, we halted and formed in line of battle.[121]

While we were forming our line, Generals Hovey and McGinnis rode forward and saw a battery on the hill, located so as to rake the road. The artillery men were lounging on their guns and saw our generals but made no attempt to shoot them. When they returned to our regiment, which was formed across the road, a lot of the boys were killing chickens and pigs. When General Hovey saw this he dashed up in a sputtering excitement, yelling to the boys, "Get into ranks quick—what, what, what the devil do you mean, foraging right here in the face of the enemy—get in ranks quick." The boys were hungry and did not pay much attention to him. Then General McGinnis came up and said very cooly, "Boys, get to your places, you will soon have bigger game than that to capture." The boys then dropped their chickens and sprang into their places in ranks, for when old Pap McGinnis (as I called him) spoke in that way, we knew there was going to be something doing right now. We immediately threw out a company as skirmishers and they drove the rebel skirmishers back, really making a charge on them. There were a number of rebel sharpshooters high in the trees, trying to shoot our officers. Our skirmishers discovered this and shot them out of the trees, where they hit the ground pretty hard when they tumbled down, but I do not think it hurt them much.

The ravine that lay between where we formed our line of battle and the hill occupied by the enemy was covered with timber and the

---

[121] General Hovey's Division, including the 11th Indiana, arrived at the Champion House about 9:45 A.M. on 16 May. The Federals delayed their attack until 10:30 before advancing against the Confederate batteline (Bearss, *Vicksburg Campaign*, vol. 2, 593–96).

hill also was timbered. Company E was at the extreme right of our regiment and my company G joined it on the left. When we moved forward in line of battle, company E was on the right of the road and my company was on the left. We left the road clear as we knew the rebel battery was placed to rake the road. They also could have seen us much sooner in the road than they could in the timber. This road ran West to the top of the hill and there it made a complete elbow and turned directly South in order to round the head of a deep gulch beyond. Right at this elbow the rebel battery was located, the guns pointing East to rake the road from Jackson. The hillside was quite steep but we charged up it. The battery held its fire until we came in sight at the crest of the hill and close to the battery, when they turned their volley loose at us. As luck would have it, they shot a second too soon and the shot went over our heads. They saw my company on the left of the road and hurriedly turned one gun to rake it. In their haste they had pointed it directly at a big hickory tree and the whole load of grape and cannister went into this tree. As this gun was not fired as soon as the others, it would have torn my company to pieces had it not been for this tree. It almost cut the tree in two. We were at the guns before they could reload but the men in that battery were as brave a set as I have ever seen. They stood to their guns until we had killed, or left for dead, every one of them. There were three brigades of infantry supporting this battery. They received our charge and we came together in deadly combat.

I have heard and read of hand-to-hand battles, and I have seen many men bayonetted and killed with the club of the gun, but this was the only real hand-to-hand battle I saw during the war. We were stabbing with bayonets, clubbing with guns, officers shooting with revolvers and slashing and thrusting with swords. I was impressed with the wicked, or I should say desperate, fighting of one fellow. We got mixed some in the charge and destruction of the battery-men, and this fellow was near me in our hand-to-hand conflict. He was about six feet and a half tall, raw-boned and muscular. He was what we called a brag as he was always blowing about how he would kill rebels by the bucketful if he could get the chance at them. Of course, he was put on the coward list with all the rest of the "blowhards," but this fellow proved an exception to the rule. He was a little to my right and about six feet in front of the rebel ranks. He had hold of the barrel of his gun and was wielding it like an Irishman with a shillelagh. He had busted the heads of a half dozen rebels who were lying dead at his feet and as he was swinging his gun to smash the head of another, a rebel nearby plunged a bayonet clear through him and he fell dead on the bodies of those he had slain. We finally broke the line in front of our regiment. When they broke, they rushed into the gulch for protection from our fire. We swung our right and left wings around so we had an encircling fire on them and we mowed them down by the hundreds. They were really piled on top of each other.[122]

There was a small stream of water in the gulch and it looked like a brook of blood. This gulch emptied into a deep ravine running at right angles with the gulch. We drove the enemy across this ravine and over the hill on the other side. We halted at the crest of the hill. As soon as the regiment halted at the top, I went forward on the ridge to see if I could locate the enemy. When I got to the far side of the ridge I could see Pemberton's whole army, that is, his reserve and wagon train and his headquarters. I saw him mounted on a horse with a group of officers around him and saw thousands of troops with guns glistening in the sun, coming on the double quick to surround us.

---

[122] The attack by the 11th Indiana and the rest of the brigade drove the Confederates from their front and enabled them to capture four cannon. By about 1:30 P.M., however, this phase of the Battle of Champion Hill was over, and the Confederates reformed their units to give battle to the Federals later that afternoon (Bearss, *Vicksburg Campaign*, vol. 2, 599–601).

They were in a broad valley and from my position I could see all over the valley. We had cut our way a half mile or more inside the rebel line, as the troops on our right and left had not been able to break the line and were still fighting in our rear where we broke the line. We took many prisoners but as none of our men would leave the front to conduct the prisoners to the rear, we would make the prisoners throw down their guns and ordered them to go to the rear. The result was that most of them moved either to the right or left and fell in with their own troops. From my viewing position on the ridge I ran back to the regiment and reported to the colonel what I had seen and informed him that we were being surrounded by a large force.

Our line of battle was facing west. As soon as I reported to my Colonel (Dan Macaully [sic]) that we were being surrounded, he ordered Colonel Bringherst [sic], commanding the 46th Indiana Infantry, and who had followed us as support, to form his regiment on our right, facing north so as to protect our right flank.[123] As soon as I had reported to my colonel what I had seen, I ran back to my point of observation and by this time the enemy were getting very close and the bullets were buzzing like a swarm of bees. I saw the enemy were coming sixteen deep. I rushed back to the right of the regiment and found Colonel Bringherst and his regiment apparently bewildered. They reminded me of a flock of ducks in a hail storm. The enemy was getting close and their bullets very profuse. I rushed

---

[123] Daniel Macauley, born in New York City in 1839, was a bookbinder in Indianapolis when the war began. Originally a first lieutenant in Company E, 11th Indiana (three months), he was quickly promoted to adjutant of the regiment. When the 11th Indiana was reorganized, Macauley served successively as adjutant, major, lieutenant colonel, and colonel. He ended the war as a brevet brigadier general for his services at the Battle of Cedar Creek. After the war he was a hotel proprietor and US Treasury Department clerk. He died in Managua, Nicaragua, in 1894 and is buried in Arlington National Cemetery (Terrell, *Report of the Adjutant General,* vol. 2, 27, 29, 75; Roger D. Hunt and Jack R. Brown, *Brevet Brigadier Generals in Blue* [Gaithersburg MD: Olde Soldier Books, 1990] 371). He was described as "a man of respectable attainments, and of more than ordinary intellect," and "an enthusiastic and gallant soldier, fierce and daring and dashing upon the battle field" (*Indianapolis Daily Journal,* 3 October 1862).

up to Colonel Bringherst with drawn sword, cursed him and threatened him and ordered him to get his regiment up to the brink of the
hill to our right and hold it or we would all be prisoners in less than
ten minutes. I practically drove him up the hill. I then saw about a
half dozen of his officers huddled behind a big tree. I rushed to them
and threatened to split their heads with my sword if they did not get
up the hill to their places. I drove them up the hill but to my disgust
the whole regiment came pellmell down the hill again in about a
minute after they took their stand. I must say that the men of the
regiment showed more bravery than did many of their officers. As
soon as Colonel Macauley saw the 46th fall back, he gave us the order
to fire and fall back. This order means to fire and load your gun as
you walk back, then turn and fire and continue to load and fire as you
fall back. Our object was to fall back to the line of battle where we
had captured the battery and cut through the line of the enemy.

We were almost entirely surrounded and the enemy was sixteen
deep in our front and demanding our surrender. When we would see
them preparing to charge, we would raise a yell to make them think
our reinforcements were coming and that would make them afraid to
charge for fear of running into a large body of troops. We doggedly
contested every foot of the ground back to where we had captured
the battery. We halted here with a resolve to die before we would back
another step. About this time our reinforcements came up but there
was such a hailstorm of bullets from the enemy that regiment after
regiment fell back as soon as the galling fire would strike them,
notwithstanding the shattered remnant of our regiment was between
them and the enemy. Finally the 17th Iowa came up and stood their
ground, then other regiments followed and the enemy was soon in
full retreat and we were relieved. Our color-bearer and the ten color-
guards were shot down and as soon as one carrying the colors fell
another guard would grab them and keep them floating in the hail of

bullets. The last guard, a member of my company, fell just as we reached the point where we had captured the battery. Colonel Macauley snatched the colors from the guard as he fell and wrapped them around his own body. No sooner than this he fell with two bad wounds, although they did not prove to be fatal.[124]

In this battle we lost very nearly one-half of our regiment in killed and wounded. I took fifty-two men of my company in the battle and lost twenty-four in killed and wounded.[125] I received several wounds in my clothes but none in my body. I cheered the boys in this battle until I could make a noise no louder than a wheeze and could not speak above a whisper for several days after. Of course, I placed myself liable to courtmartial and dishonorable dismissal from the army by cursing Colonel Bringherst [sic], a superior officer. But I had sworn I would die fighting rather than surrender and be made a prisoner and when I saw such a vast army surrounding us I thought the time had come for a showdown. I knew I would not surrender so I became as near being excited as I ever did in my life, in fact, I believe I was so excited that I would have whacked the Colonel as quickly as I would a cowardly soldier. But I never heard a word in regard to the matter. I was satisfied the Colonel had no desire to have the facts exposed before a courtmartial.

The 46th Indiana did some good fighting during the war but they appeared to have lost their nerve that day and I think the main

---

[124] At 2:30 P.M., 5,000 Confederates counterattacked the Federals, drove them off Champion Hill, captured two Union guns, and recaptured two of the artillery pieces lost earlier in the day. As soon as three fresh Federal brigades and some massed artillery halted the Confederate drive, however, Hovey's division, including the 11th Indiana, reentered the battle. By nightfall the Confederates had withdrawn from the field (Bearss, *Vicksburg Campaign,* vol. 2, 609–16).

[125] Brigadier General George F. McGinnis's Brigade suffered the heaviest losses of any Union brigade at Champion Hill (619), with 90 men killed, 506 wounded, and 23 missing at the end of the fighting. The 11th Indiana suffered 167 casualties, the second highest regimental loss in the brigade, while Colonel T. H. Bringhurst's 46th Indiana, the regiment Durham attempted to move, lost 69 men (Bearss, *Vicksburg Campaign,* vol. 2, 646–51).

trouble was they had some poor officers in the regiment. While we were falling back, a little Dutchman in my company received a scalp wound that knocked him down. The enemy was close to us, the shot addled him and he started back on all fours while the rebels were hollering at him to surrender and sending a storm of bullets at him, but he kept going until he got in our rear. He then got to his feet, snatched a gun from beside a dead soldier and rushed back with bayonet fixed and crying like a child, yelling "Durham, Durham, them damned rebels tried to kill me and damn them they have got my hat." I saw he was addled and would have rushed right into the ranks of the enemy and make a fight for his hat. I caught him and he soon came to his senses and finished the fight hatless. It was a close call for him as it was a bad scalp wound. I told him the only reason he was not killed was because his skull was so thick the bullet could not penetrate it. We lost many of our best men of the company in this battle. I will never forget the look little Cy Bair gave me when he fell by my side, shot through the neck and the jugular vein cut. It was while we were falling back, and we had no time to carry anyone off the field. His life's blood was spurting from the wound and he knew he was passing into the great mysterious beyond; he gave me such an imploring look that it was forever stamped upon my memory. I love[d] the orphan boy and he thought the world of me. He looked on me as a father. I hated to see him go worse than most anyone who gave up their lives for their country's honor. There was no braver boy lived than he.[126] •

---

[126] The Indiana Adjutant General's Report states that Private Cyrus H. Bair of Montgomery County died on 19 May 1863 of wounds received at Champion Hill. He had enlisted with the original members of the company on 31 August 1861. Bair is buried in grave 3673, section O, of the Vicksburg National Cemetery. He was one of four members of Company G who were killed outright or died of wounds at Champion Hill (Terrell, *Report of the Adjutant General*, vol. 4, 189–90).

I had a fellow in my company was in the habit of falling out of ranks in battle and would prowl over the battle field and rob the dead. When we were starting into this battle I told the orderly to see that the company kept in line and that I was going to stop this fellow from robbing the dead. I got behind him with my revolver in hand, intending to shoot him down the first move he made to leave the ranks; but in our charge on the battery and our hand-to-hand combat, I forgot all about my man. So he got away and followed up his vocation. It was two or three days before he showed up. He claimed he had charged through the rebel line, was taken prisoner and two guards were taking him to the rear and he killed both the guards and took two fine revolvers from them which he displayed with much gusto. After he had killed the guards he charged through the rebel line on the south and came out to the Union line in front of General Osterhouse's [sic] division. I concluded this lie entitled him to live, but he died not long afterward. In writing of the death of my little friend, Cy. Bair, I neglected to mention the fact that we saw the rebel who shot Bair. Joe Hanna was near Bair when he was shot and saw the rebel, who was a big fellow, level his gun on Bair. Hanna shot almost at the same instant and the rebel dropped dead at the same time Bair did.

The fact is that our division under General Alvin P. Hovey of Indiana, did nearly all the fighting at Champions Hill where the rebel General Pemberton's army of near fifty thousand were defeated. General Logan's division did a little fighting on our right. General McPherson reinforced us with a portion of his corps after the hardest of the fighting was over. All told there were not 15,000 Union troops engaged in this battle. Hovey lost, in killed and wounded, over one-third of his division which is almost unprecedented for a division.[127]

---

[127] Hovey's Division suffered 198 killed, 872 wounded, and 119 missing, for a total of 1,189. To put this figure in perspective, nearly half the casualties suffered by the Union army in the Battle of Champion Hill came from Hovey's Division. Major General John A. Logan's 3rd Division, 17th Army Corps lost 406 casualties (Bearss, *Vicksburg Campaign*, vol. 2, 642, 647–48).

As our division had suffered such a great loss in this battle, it was left to care for the wounded and bury the dead while the other troops followed the enemy. We worked all night the night of the 16th carrying the wounded off the field to the field hospital, which was nothing but a canvas stretched in the woods near the battle field.

The battle did not end until about 4:00 p.m. and we were in constant deadly combat for about five hours. We had about finished getting the wounded off the field the evening of the 17th and on the 18th I was ordered to take command of a detail of about 100 men and gather the dead and the arms off the field and bury the dead. I procured a big cotton wagon with three yokes of oxen to pull it. This wagon held as much as four or five ordinary wagons. I put some of the men to digging two long ditches running east and west near the Vicksburg-Jackson road where the heaviest fighting had been done. We piled the dead and the guns we gathered from the field in this wagon all together. We hauled them to the ditches, unloaded them on the ground where part of the detail separated them and threw the rebels in the south ditch and the Union men in the north ditch. After we had the ditches filed [sic] to within about two and a half feet of the surface we covered them up. We threw the guns and accoutrements in a pile which was turned over to the quartermaster general. In battle one saw the enemy slain by thousands and even saw his own comrades fall around him, with little feeling; but after the battle, to see the wounded and mangled suffering is sickening and heartrending. At this field hospital I saw many wagonloads of hands, feet, legs and arms piled in heaps higher than my head. Nor is carrying the wounded from the field a pleasant task. The groans of the dying, the begging for help and begging for a sip of water, and begging to be taken from the field at once where they could get medical aid, after lying on the ground for twenty-four or perhaps forty-eight hours of intense pain in a pool of their own life blood, was terrible. They not only suffered from their wounds but from the cold or the hot sun.

These scenes called forth all the human sympathy the heart possessed—you want to carry all from the field at once and relieve their suffering, but you cannot, and when you pass them by you can hear them sobbing from disappointment and a feeling they had been neglected and inhumanly treated. In gathering the wounded from the field it is human nature to care for your own immediate comrades; in doing this you have to pass by hundreds who are imploring you to take them. Then again, it is human nature to care for your own wounded first before caring for the enemy, though when our own were cared for we cared for the enemy's wounded with the same tender care we gave our own comrades.

In gathering up the wounded from this battlefield I saw what impressed me as queer consolation. There was a little black-eyed surgeon of the rebel army who was caring for the wounded, he had procured an old bench and was using it as an operating table. He had a couple of his soldiers with him and with a stretcher they would carry the men whom he had selected to his operating bench. The surgeon was strictly business. His shirt sleeves were rolled up above his elbows and he was covered with blood from head to foot. As he was taking a man to his operating bench he passed near one of his wounded soldiers who said, "Oh doctor, you must do something for me quick, I can't stand this any longer." The surgeon, without halting, said to the soldier, "Now be patient, just be patient, and I will be back in a minute and cut your leg off for you."

Right where the battery stood that we captured in our first charge on Champion's Hill, I found a small bush that had forked in six prongs about three and a half feet above the ground. All of these branches had been cut off by bullets. I dug the bush up and made a cane out of it for my father. About noon on the 19th, having finished burying all the dead we could find on the battle field, we started for Vicksburg.

Before leaving, the Colonel was ordered to leave one of our regimental surgeons to look after the wounded of our regiment. Rockwell, the hospital steward, with whom I had the racket at Paducah, Kentucky, and who in the meantime had been promoted to 3d assistant surgeon, was left to look after the comfort of the wounded of our regiment. As soon as we left, he began amputating the arms and legs of our wounded without the knowledge or consent of either the brigade division or corps surgeons who were responsible for the surgery. Of course everyone this villain operated on died. He amputated limbs where they had just flesh wounds and the bone had not been touched. As soon as the commanding surgeon found this out he ordered the cur to hand him his resignation at once or he would have him arrested and dishonorably dismissed from the service. The villain sent in his resignation but he was too smart to show himself around the regiment, for as soon as we heard of his infernal work he would have been torn to pieces if he had ever come near the regiment again. But he skipped for home and that knocked me out of a chance to get evened up with him. I saw in the adjutant general's report where he died in Junction City, Kansas long years ago, so all the chance left for me to get even with the villain was to say "curses to his memory."[128]

Before closing the account of this battle of Champion's Hill, I wish to make mention of Bob Mathews [sic] of my company who was a color guard in this battle. He received eight wounds while we were being forced back to where we captured the battery. He was the

---

[128] William Rockwell resigned from the army and was discharged as assistant surgeon based on a surgeon's certificate that stated he was suffering from "chronic diarrhea." At the time of his death in Rockwell City (Norton County) KS on 18 September 1884, Rockwell was still suffering from that complaint in addition to a "continual hacking cough" (William Rockwell pension record, RG 15, National Archives and Records Administration, Washington, DC).

last of the guards to fall. It was when he fell that Colonel Macaully grabbed the colors up and wrapped them around his body. Of the eight wounds Mathews received, one ball went directly through his breast, passing clear through his body. After the battle we carried him to the field hospital and laid him on the ground under a fig tree, expecting him to die in a few minutes. We paid no more attention to him as we were busy carrying those wounded who had some show of living. The next day we went to get Mathews and bury him with the others of our company who had been killed and to our astonishment we found him still alive. He got well and was made captain of a company and served the remainder of the war and lived many years after the war.[129]

On the morning of the 21st we were in front of the fortifications at Vicksburg. We were skirmishing all day and from that time on until the surrender of Vicksburg at 9:00 o'clock [sic] a.m. July 4, 1863, it was a continuous battle.

The sharpshooters entertained the enemy while others were sapping and mining, that is, digging rifle pits toward the forts of the enemy. The country back of Vicksburg where the forts were located was broken and rough, composed of ridges and ravines. In many of the ravines were canebreaks. We did our sleeping and eating in these ravines where we were shielded from the shot of the enemy. We made sap rollers ahead of us to shield us from the sight of the enemy and from their bullets. These trenches were dug deep enough so a man could walk erect in them and his head could not be seen by the enemy. In approaching the forts of the enemy with these trenches we did not dig them in a direct line but would zig-zag so that the side of

---

[129] Robert W. Matthews of Thorntown IN enlisted in Company G on 31 August 1861. He was commissioned a first lieutenant in the company in January 1865, then captain of Company C the following month. He was mustered out with the regiment in July 1865 (Terrell, *Report of the Adjutant General*, vol. 2, 78, 81; vol. 4, 189).

our trench or rifle pits would be toward the enemy. We finally got our rifle pits up to within seventy-five feet of the fort in front of us. We could throw rocks or clods of dirt over into their fort.[130]

Immediately in front of these forts the enemy had a large ditch dug about eight feet deep and twelve feet wide. This ditch was filled with soldiers to contest an assault on the fort. Our rifle pits ran parallel with the front of the fort. On the front or side of our rifle pits fronting the enemy, we placed large logs or bags of cotton. Underneath these we had portholes just large enough to receive a gun barrel. The enemy had the same on their forts. For weeks we would watch these port holes in the fort of the enemy and when we would see one darkened we knew someone was in front of it and would fire at the port hole. The same rule was observed by the enemy, in fact both sides kept up a constant fire at these port holes. Many lost their lives by having the curiosity to peep thru the port holes. We killed two rebel generals who were taking a peep at us through these holes.[131] I used to tremble for General Grant when he would come into our rifle pits and take a squint at the enemy through the holes. He would no sooner get in front of one than a volley of shots would be fired at it from the enemy but luckily none hit the target. We had much sport with the rebels when we were close to their fort. They were quite hungry and we would throw crackers on the side of their fort. The soldiers in the big trench in front of the fort would reach up for them and we would shoot at their hands. They soon got onto this trick and would use sticks or poles to rake the crackers down, but

---

[130] A War Department historical marker erected to honor Hovey's Division at Vicksburg National Military Park claims that the division was located within about thirty-five feet of the ditch of Confederate Fort Garrott (Henry C. Adams Jr., *Indiana at Vicksburg* [Indianapolis: Wm. B. Burford, 1911] 73).

[131] Confederate Colonel Isham W. Garrott was killed on 17 June 1863, about three weeks after his promotion to brigadier general, although word of his new rank had not yet reached Vicksburg. General Martin E. Green was killed on the morning of 27 June 1863 (Bearss, *Vicksburg Campaign*, vol. 3, 903–904, 941).

they could not tell just when their hands would be in sight of our boys who were watching to send a volley at them the moment a hand was in sight. This was a little like the sport the boys had with the frogs, as related in our old readers—it was fun for the boys but rough on the frogs.

Many queer things were done there that were not usually done by belligerents. For instance, when we would put our night pickets out, both sides put them out at the same time. We agreed with the enemy that at picket time all firing should cease the moment the officer of the day on either side stepped on top of the works in full uniform and there would be no shot fired after that until the last picket was inside their works. In the morning, their officers and ours would walk side by side in establishing the pickets, each instructing their pickets not to converse with the picket of the enemy. But they did all the same, as they were stationed so close together they could have punched each other with their bayonets. We agreed with those in front of us that we would have no picket fighting in the night. The result was that their officers and ours would meet between the lines on a mound a little to our left and have a general good time at night. We would furnish the whiskey and they the tobacco and cigars. Sometimes there would be as many as fifty officers of both sides sitting there together, cracking jokes and telling stor[i]es. The rest of us would watch the shells thrown from our mortar boats.[132]

These shells weighed four to six hundred pounds each and were thrown into the city night and day all during the siege. Some would fall to the ground and burst, while many would burst high up in the air above the city and the fragments rain down on the city. They were a beautiful sight at night as they had a rotary motion while the fuze

---

[132] Six Union scows, each armed with a 13-inch mortar, arrived opposite Vicksburg and began shelling the city on 20 May 1863. Some 7,000 of these 200-pound shells were fired into Vicksburg before the Confederates surrendered (Bearss, *Vicksburg Campaign*, vol. 3, 711, 1249, 1273).

was in a blaze. The rebel officers said they called the shells "baby wakers" in Vicksburg. Often while we would be sitting there having a good time, a night battle would break loose not far from us and we would sit and enjoy the beauties of it together. A night battle is a beautiful sight when one can see it without being a participant in it. Quite a friendship formed among the officers at these meetings. One officer I met there was an adjutant of a Georgia regiment. His name was Green and he was a grandson of old General Green [sic] of the Revolution.[133] After these friendly visits at night, the moment the last picket was in his works in the morning, firing would open up and continue all day until picket time at night. Of course this was after we got so close to their forts. Before this we had picket fighting all night. When we got close to their works we told the enemy it would decide nothing to shoot pickets at night, that it took battles to decide the issue and they readily agreed with us, but many places along the line on either side of us, where they were not in such close proximity, they fought all night.

Our boys would josh the rebels across the line at night with such questions as, "Hello Johnnie, how are you off for grub? Better come over and get a square meal. How do you like mule meat as a dessert anyhow? We are coming in the 4th of July to celebrate with you," etc. Not knowing how truly they were speaking—I believe it was partly on account of so many of the boys telling them they were going into Vicksburg the 4th to celebrate that caused Pemberton to open up capitulation on the 3d, and I think it was Grant's intention to assault

---

[133] Possibly Lieutenant Samuel Percival Greene. A native of South Carolina, Greene served as adjutant of the 39th Georgia Infantry, a part of Brigadier General Alfred Cumming's Brigade, located near the 11th Indiana's position. After his surrender and parole at Vicksburg, Greene finally surrendered and was paroled at Greensboro NC on 1 May 1865, as a captain (Gen. Clement A. Evans, ed., *Confederate Military History*, vol. 15 [Atlanta: Confederate Publishing Co., 1899; reprint, Wilmington NC: Broadfoot Publishing Company, 1988] 427–29; Compiled Service Records of Confederate Soldiers Who Served in Organizations From the State of Georgia, microcopy 266, roll 443, National Archives, Washington, DC).

the works on the 4th, had they not surrendered.[134] One night one of our boys got to joshing a rebel across the line and found out the rebel was his father. The next night the father deserted and came across to his son.

The rebel army in Vicksburg were nearly started [starved] when they surrendered as we had them surrounded so they could get no provisions into the city. They had lived on mule meat for weeks and as the feed for the mules had given out, the mules were very poor and most of them had been killed and eaten. General Pemberton knew he could not hold out longer; he knew his soldiers were starving and ready to mutiny and throw down their arms. He knew there would be little resistance if we assaulted on the 4th as he expected, and General Grant well knew the condition and feeling of the army in Vicksburg.

When we first invested Vicksburg our signal corps had a lookout in a very large oak tree. They bored holes in the trunk of the tree and drove wooden pins in the holes so they could climb the tree.[135] I had a great desire to see how Vicksburg really looked so I got a field glass and climbed the tree. As I was anxious for a good look I wished to climb to the very top of the tree. There were no wooden pins for a foot hold above the first limbs and the trunk was so large I could climb no higher without taking my boots off. As there were about a dozen soldiers in the boughs of the tree at the time I took my boots off, I put them far out on a big limb where I thought they could neither see nor climb to them. They were almost new boots that I had made at home and sent to me. I knew half of our army were bare-footed so I took extra pains to hide them out of sight far out on the

---

[134] Actually Grant issued orders for a 6 July assault on the rebel fortifications (Bearss, *Vicksburg Campaign*, vol. 3, 953).

[135] A postwar map drawn by C. J. Durham shows a "larger tree west of Gen[.] Hoveys [sic] Hd Qrs where holes were bored and pins were driven for a lookout or Signal Station" (11th Indiana File, Vicksburg National Military Park Library).

limb. I then climbed clear to the top of the tree, higher than I think anyone had ever climbed. I then turned my glasses on the city. I could see all over the city and became greatly interested and it was not long until some fool rebel opened up on me with solid shot from a cannon. His first shot went rather wild, his next shot was better range, and the third shot came crashing through the top of the tree close by me, cutting off a lot of limbs that reminded me that I had seen all I cared to at this time, so I concluded to move my quarters. I then looked down for the first time and to my surprise there was not a man left in the tree. I climbed down to the limb where I had hidden my boots and to my chagrin they also had disappeared. I had too much confidence in my boots to accuse them of cowardice, so I concluded someone had seen me hide them and had taken them. For quite a while after that I inspected the feet of every fellow I would meet. I knew being barefoot I was not entirely out of fashion. I found a sutler who had an extra pair of shoes—the only extra pair to be found in the whole army here. I planked down my last five dollars in gold and took the shoes. The fit was not considered.

One day I took three or four of my men with me and went up a ravine toward the works of the enemy. At the head of this ravine there was a perpendicular bluff about eight feet high. I got the boys to help me onto this bluff and I was then on top of a ridge that ran at right angles. I put my field glasses to my eyes to see what there was beyond the ridge and just as I was getting a good look, about twenty Johnnies, who were concealed about twenty-five yards in front of me, fired a volley at me. One bullet struck the hilt of my sword and another went through my clothes but missed my body. The boys below me heard the ball strike my sword and supposed I was killed. It took me very little time to make up my mind that I had seen all I wished to see from that point so I jumped down over the bluff. The boys were surprised to see me jump down instead of roll down.

One day I was scouting around between our works and that of the enemy. A shell from our mortar guns burst high up in the air and half of the shell came in a curve right at me. I was sure it would drive me into the ground and on account of its curvature I could not determine to a nicety just where it would strike but it looked like it was coming right down on my head. I feared to step to one side for fear I would step right where it would strike so I set my teeth with the resolve to meet my fate like a true soldier, feeling certain that I was a goner, but fortunately for me it struck the ground about four feet from me and was buried in the ground. These shells were larger than a bushel basket and made a fearful report when they burst high in the air. It was during this siege a rebel officer jumped up on top of a fort about one hundred yards from our rifle pits. He was brandishing his sword and cursing the Yankees. He shook his sword and fist at us. We thought he was coming over to lick our whole army single handed. After he raved a while the boys concluded to stop his violent exercise but a gunner from our battery asked to let him try a bomb shot at the fellow. When the gunner fired the ball it struck the fellow midway of the body and bursted him like a glass ball. I have never seen pieces of flesh fly in so many directions as I saw there. It looked as though he was blown into mincemeat. I think the shell exploded just as it struck him.

Early in the morning of July 4th, the day of the surrender, we received orders to draw five days' rations and to prepare at once to move against General Joseph E. Johnson [sic] who was in our rear with a large army. There was a barrel of whiskey issued to our regiment the morning of the 4th. I got two canteens of whiskey and my five days' rations and as soon as the surrender was made I started to the city. After trying so long to get into the city I did not propose to leave there until I'd seen the inside.

The 2d Texas Rangers were in our front.[136] We watched them
march outside their works, form in line, their band played honors to
their colors, then they stacked their arms. It was one of the most
solemn and affecting scenes I have ever beheld. There was no
outburst of rejoicing on our part. In fact the scene was so solemn that
nearly every one of our soldiers shed tears. As soon as they had
stacked arms I went to the regiment and was met by the surgeon of
the regiment. He was somewhat intoxicated and he shook hands with
me and introduced himself by saying, "Well Captain, I am from Texas
by G—. I suppose you want to see the city and I will pilot you
through." I told him that was just what I wished to see. I then handed
him one of my canteens and told him to drink hearty, which he did
without any insistence on my part. We then started to town. I told
him I first wished to see the boys that were left of the battery we took
at Champion's Hill. He took me to their camp.

I think there were just five of them that had gotten away alive. I
told the battery boys I wanted to "set 'em up" to them for standing to
their guns so gallantly at Champion's Hill, so I gave them my two
canteens of whiskey and my five days' rations of grub and I doubt if
they ever appreciated a treat more than they did this one, for they
were almost starved. Then the gentleman from Texas piloted me
through the city. It was interesting, if not amusing, to see the women
in hysterics, raving, pulling their hair, stamping their feet and cursing
the Yankees. They seemed to think the world had come to an end and
they wanted to die hard, but they mellowed down a little when we
began to feed them. We not only fed the army that had surrendered
but all the citizens of the city, for they were all quite hungry when the
surrender was made. As I have said, the ground on which Vicksburg

---

[136] Possibly the 2nd Texas Infantry Battalion of Colonel Thomas N. Waul's Texas Legion Infantry
Regiment. Waul's Legion was assigned to Major General Carter L. Stevenson's Division during the siege
(Bearss, *Vicksburg Campaign*, vol. 3, 964–65).

stands was very broken and rough; the earth is of a nature that will not crumble or cave easily and during the siege most of the families had dug out rooms in the hillsides and banks and lived in these underground rooms to protect themselves from our shells. Many of these underground rooms were furnished as well as one would see in the finest houses. There was hardly a house in the city that was not riddled by our cannon balls and shells.

As soon as the enemy surrendered and stacked their arms, the Union and rebel soldiers fraternized as if they had been fighting for the same cause.[137] There was no enmity shown by either side.

---

[137] Samuel L. Ensminger of the 11th Indiana wrote that on the morning of 4 July 1863, after the Confederates had stacked their arms, Union troops went among the rebels for a couple of hours, had a "social session," and divided their rations with them (Dr. Samuel L. Ensminger to Captain William T. Rigby, Crawfordsville IN, 22 August 1907, 11th Indiana File, Vicksburg National Military Park Library).

Chapter 7

JACKSON AND FURLOUGH

On the morning of the 5th of July we started to pay our respects to the army of Joseph E. Johnson [sic]. The weather was very hot and dry. We bivouacked at the Black River bridge that night and on the 7th we crossed Black River on the railroad bridge and marched by way of Edwards station and Champion's Hill to Bolton on the Jackson and Vicksburg railroad. Johnson's [sic] army was stationed here but retreated in the direction of Jackson after some hard skirmishing. The 8th we lay at Bolton until 5:00 p.m. then marched to the Clinton road and at midnight bivouacked by the side of the road. On the 9th we marched on the railroad to Clinton. We were skirmishing with the enemy all the way from Bolton, driving the enemy before us. Some of these skirmishes should have been given the dignity of battles.

On the 10th we drove the enemy inside their entrenchments at Jackson and that night we formed our lines of battle and took our position around their breastworks, but on the 11th we moved to our right. Our division, Hovey's, took position on the left of Lowman's division. General Carr, with his division, joined our division on the left. We had pretty heavy fighting to procure this new position on our right.

The morning of the 12th we advanced in line of battle and drove the enemy inside their fortifications and that evening General Lowman [sic] assaulted the works in front of him. This assault was made without orders from the commanding general (Sherman) and Lowman got two of his regiments badly slaughtered and within two hours after the assault was relieved of his command and made to resign at once in order to avoid courtmartial.[138] On the 13th we were advanced to within seven hundred yards of the enemy's works. We kept up a lively sharp shooting fight all day. On the 14th the enemy made several sorties but were repulsed and driven back with heavy loss. We kept up a hot skirmish with the enemy on the 15th and 16th, and on the night of the 16th the enemy evacuated Jackson. We got into the city about daylight the morning of the 17th but as the enemy had left at about 2 o'clock in the night, they had too much of a start on us to overtake them with our infantry. Our cavalry followed them for about twenty miles. We took about 1000 prisoners at Jackson. From the night of the evacuation until the 21st we were busy destroying railroads and public buildings. We destroyed everything that could be of benefit to the enemy.

We started back to Vicksburg at 3:00 o'clock [sic] the morning of the 21st and got to Vicksburg at noon the 23rd. The weather was very hot and the water scarce and bad. Many of the soldiers played out and fell by the wayside. Captain Ruckle and I were the first of the regiment to reach Vicksburg, others of the regiment kept straggling in for two days. I will say here that in the Vicksburg and Jackson campaigns there was hardly a day from the morning of the first day in May until the morning of the 17th of July that I was not under fire, and a great portion of that time we had good lively fighting. We took over thirty-five thousand prisoners, 175 cannon, 65,000 muskets and a large amount of ammunition. When we crossed the Mississippi River on April 30th we had just two days' rations and did not receive

---

[138] Jacob Gartner Lauman (1813–1867) was a veteran of Belmont, Fort Donelson, and Shiloh. After his division's failed assault against the Confederate fortifications at Jackson on 12 July 1863, Lauman was relieved of command by General Edward O. C. Ord, but did not resign. Instead he reported to Grant at Vicksburg, then was directed to return to Iowa to await further orders. He did not receive another field command before the war ended (Ezra J. Warner, *Generals in Blue: Lives of the Union Commanders* [Baton Rouge: Louisiana State University Press, 1964] 275–76).

any more until we got the enemy bottled up in Vicksburg about the 23rd of May.

We lived on parched corn most of the time, which was about all we could find in the country to eat. We parched it and made coffee out of it with which to wash the dry corn down our throats. At one place where we bivouacked we found an old hand corn grinder. We ground some corn and made Johnny cakes, which we baked on a board, or in case we could find no board, we baked it in the ashes, but as this meal was not bolted and we had no salt, it was not a very inviting feast for anybody but a very hungry man. It is useless to say we were hungry and enjoyed our "hoe cakes." It is plain to be seen that we were wholly dependent on the country through which we were marching or invading, for subsistence. The enemy had appropriated to their own use all the provisions in the country, thus making our picking painfully slim. Yet, with all our starvation and hardships, marching and fighting day and night through rain and hot sunshine, there was no grumbling among the soldiers. It seemed that every soldier was determined to make the campaign a success and gladly made every sacrifice necessary to that end.

When we crossed the Mississippi River we had no wagons or any way by which we could transport our ammunition, so we sent details out through the country to gather up vehicles with which to haul our ammunition and it was equal to a circus parade in a country town to see this ammunition caravan. There were fine family carriages loaded with boxes of ammunition and drawn by an ox team, or an old mule and horse hitched together, rigged with plow harness, shuck collars and rope lines to drive with. There were cotton wagons, ox carts and even dog carts—everything that could be found in the country that had wheels, and every kind of an animal and harness with which to pull them, were pressed into service. No such sight has ever been seen since old Noah entered the Ark. It was a motley looking outfit for a well equipped army, but it answered the purpose as it enabled us to keep our ammunition with us and we used it to good advantage.

On the 29th of July General Grant gave me a thirty days' leave of absence to go home.[139] As there had been much dissatisfaction in the North with the progress of the Union army and the northern "copperheads" were growing very bold and many Union men becoming discouraged, General Grant thought it would have a good influence in the North to have a lot of our officers return home for a short time. It would encourage the Union people and discourage the "copperheads," so he gave one officer out of each company a thirty-day leave of absence to go home. He also gave a leave of absence to a proportionate number of field or general officers. This was a wise move on Grant's part for it had the desired effect, for when we, who had been in the field, told them of our victories and our determination to subdue the South before we let up on them, it was much more effective than reading conflicting accounts in the newspapers. The result was the Union men took on new courage and it was equally discouraging to the "copperheads." This far-sighted and wise move of Grant was never fully appreciated.

I left Vicksburg for home on July 29th and reached Indianapolis on August 7th and arrived home August 8th. We had a tedious trip up the Mississippi River as we got stuck on a number of sand bars and would have to work a day or two to get off. I had not yet received my commission. When the Colonel and General recommended me to Governor Oliver P. Morton of Indiana for promotion, the Governor, instead of sending me a commission as requested, sent a commission

---

[139] On 26 July 1863, Durham wrote a letter to John A. Rawlins, assistant adjutant general of the Army of the Tennessee, requesting a leave of twenty days in order to attend to "private interests" at home (Thomas Wise Durham compiled military service record, RG 94, National Archives and Records Administration, Washington, DC). Durham was not alone. A soldier in the 11th noted that "Furloughs' are all the 'rage' at the present time, both with the 'commissioned' and 'private.' Three men from a company are granted a leave of absence"(*Indianapolis Daily Journal*, 20 August 1863).

to his nephew, a recruit who did not know how to right-face a company. As soon as we arrived at Indianapolis, General McGinnis had me go with him to see Gov. Morton. The general introduced me to the Governor and told him I was the man they had recommended for a commission, that the officers in the army knew who were qualified and entitled to the positions, that I had won the promotion on the battlefields, that they had recommended me knowing I was qualified for the position and entitled to it, and that they would never muster the man he had commissioned and that I was the only man they would allow to be mustered and demanded a commission for me. He told the Governor we were staying there until he revoked the commission he had issued for the other man and issued one for me. The Governor at once revoked the other commission and wrote out a commission for me and handed it to me. And so it is seen that consanguinity sometimes cuts a large figure even with great men.

I started back to the regiment on the 24th day of August. The regiment in the meantime had been sent from Vicksburg to the Department of the Gulf at New Orleans, La. Most all the officers of Indiana regiments who were on leave of absence arranged to start back to the army on the same day. I do not think there was an officer in the whole outfit that some friend had not slipped a bottle of "O.B. Joyful" in his pocket as he entered his car to leave.[140] When we reached the Illinois state line there were three or four hundred officers on the train. It is putting it very mild when I say they were a jolly set. In Illinois our train tried to pass another train on the same track. Of course there was a collision and wreck. Several persons were killed but none of our officers were badly injured. This caused a delay of several hours.

---

[140] Soldier slang for liquor.

We arrived at Cairo, Ill., on the morning of the 27th and had to lay over a day before we could get a boat down the river. The night we stayed at Cairo there was a circus. We all marched in in perfect military order. We did not stop at the ticket box but marched into the tent and took charge of the performance. Captain Scott of our regiment took charge as ringmaster and the rest of us filled other positions and acted as ushers in seating the crowd.[141] The circus men tumbled to the situation and knew it would do no good to buck, so they would instruct us in carrying out the programme. I remember it as the best circus I have ever seen. However, I admit I may be a little partial as it was the first and only big circus that I ever helped to manage.

On the 28th we boarded a boat for down the river. We had a jolly good time on the boat. There was music, dancing and gambling. I saw two southern women indulge in a fight one night on the boat. One slashed the other with a stilletto and split one of her breasts wide open. One night I heard a racket on the cabin deck just back of my stateroom. I rushed out and found a couple of river gamblers throwing a captain of a Missouri regiment overboard. They had the captain balanced over the railing of the deck, head downward and ready to drop in the river just as I sprang to him and yanked him back. I grabbed the captain with one hand and knocked the gamblers down with the other. It was done so quickly they had no time to make a gun play and before they got to their feet I had the captain on deck and the gamblers covered with my gun. They obeyed my orders to return to their quarters. The old captain was very grateful to me for saving his life and wanted to reward me for it but as the gamblers had robbed him of every cent of his money the best he could do was to give me his photograph as a token of appreciation.

---

[141] Francis G. Scott of Terre Haute IN was commissioned a first lieutenant in Company C of the 11th in August 1861. He was promoted to captain in April 1862 and died in October 1863 (William H. H. Terrell, *Report of the Adjutant General of the State of Indiana*, vol. 2 [Indianapolis: W. R. Holloway, 1865] 78).

Chapter 8

NEW ORLEANS AND WESTERN LOUISIANA

We arrived at New Orleans on September 9th. We were hung up on sand bars many times on our way down the river. We found our regiment camped at New Orleans. General Nathaniel P. Banks of Ohio was in command of the Department of the Gulf, having succeeded General Ben Butler.[142] At this time all the troops in the Department of the Gulf were Eastern troops except the 21st Indiana heavy artillery and a Wisconsin regiment. There was not any great affinity at that time between the Eastern and Western troops for the Eastern army under General George B. McLelland [sic] had been "marching up the hill and down again" ever since the war began and had accomplished nothing.[143] While we knew it was the fault of the commander and not the soldiers, yet as they upheld McLelland [sic] with such ardor and claimed he was the greatest general on earth or in Heaven, it caused us to have rather a disgust for all Eastern troops. Nor did it

---

[142] Nathaniel Prentiss Banks (1816–1894), a native of Massachusetts and former governor of that state, was appointed a major general of volunteers when the war began. Banks was defeated while in command of Union troops at the Battle of Cedar Mountain VA in August 1862, but was appointed to command the Department of the Gulf that December. He captured the Confederate stronghold of Port Hudson LA in July, then embarked on a campaign to move Federal forces into Texas. His disastrous Red River Campaign against Shreveport the following year effectively ended his military career (Patricia L. Faust, ed., *Historical Times Illustrated Encyclopedia of the Civil War* [New York: Harper Collins Publishers, 1986] 38).

[143] George Brinton McClellan (1826–1885), a graduate of West Point and veteran of the Mexican War, was given command of the Army of the Potomac after the First Battle of Bull Run. Turned back in a drive for Richmond VA (the Peninsula Campaign) from March to August 1862, McClellan defeated Robert E. Lee's first invasion of the North at Antietam later that year. Relieved of command by President Abraham Lincoln, McClellan accepted the Democratic presidential nomination in 1864 and was defeated by his former commander-in-chief (Faust, *Historical Times Illustrated Encyclopedia*, 456).

detract from this feeling when we got to New Orleans and found all the officers of the Eastern troops rigged out in white kid gauntlets reaching to the elbow, and wearing white starched linen shirts, and a profusion of plumes and cockades. The private soldiers were rigged out in white paper collars and white cotton gloves. Their "excelsior" dress gave them a feeling of superiority over us to such an extent that their private soldiers would not even recognize our officers. True, we were rather rough looking citizens, having been in the campaign and trenches around Vicksburg and Jackson for months. We had not quite got all the mud off our clothes when we landed at New Orleans but we felt as proud of what we had accomplished as our Eastern friends did of their clothes, and inasmuch as we felt that we were their equals in every respect and superiors in some, we knew it would be an honor for them to get acquainted with us. Therefore, we at once began introducing ourselves by giving them lessons in the fine art of pugilism. If a squad of our officers stepped into a saloon or other resort and found it filled with Eastern officers we would at once proceed to knock them down and drag them out. No ceremonies were necessary and the soldiers of our regiment gave the same lessons to the Eastern soldiers.

In these little friendly scraps for recognition, the other officers of my regiment dubbed me "old power," for the fact that I was stouter and a better athlete than any of the other officers.

Sometimes when we would meet up with a gang of Eastern officers and indulge in the little "introductory formalities," our officers would hold me in reserve until the Eastern fellows were about to get the better of the introduction and then someone of our fellows who was getting the worst of it would yell, "turn old power loose." Sufficient to say it was not long until they learned to give us consideration. Yet in a talk with them one day they said they were willing to acknowledge that the Western troops could do brute fighting but they could not drill. We told them to pick their crack regiment and name the amount of money they wanted to drill for and we would cover it any given time and have a contest drill. When we called their hand so readily they felt a little suspicious and began to try to find out our history. The result was they backed out. We then gave notice through the city paper (The Picaune) [sic] that we would give a parade drill in the city park on a certain day. We gave the drill and all the Eastern soldiers and officers that were camped near the city were out to see the drill. All the generals were out, including General Banks, Franklin and Thomas, who was then Adjutant General of the United States.[144] After we got through with our drill, General Thomas made us a speech in which he said he had seen all the crack regiments of this country and of most every other country in the world drill and had never seen any that could equal us in drill. General Banks also made us a very laudatory speech, declaring the world could not equal us in proficiency in drill and the manual of arms.

That night General Banks gave all the officers of our regiment a champagne supper, which I learned cost him five hundred dollars. The Easterners admitted that we could beat them drilling but said the old New York 7th regiment could beat us.[145] But the rivalry between the Eastern and Western troops had not yet died out. So far we had

---

[144] General Nathaniel Banks commanded the Department of the Gulf (roughly comprising the coast of the Gulf of Mexico from west Florida to Texas), from December 1862 to September 1864, while General William B. Franklin led the 19th Army Corps in that department (Frank J. Welcher, *The Union Army, 1861–1865*, vol. 2 [Bloomington: Indiana University Press, 1989] 29–30, 317). Lorenzo Thomas was adjutant general of the United States from 1861 to 1869, and was in the field for most of 1863 inspecting armies, posts, and operations (Welcher, *Union Army*, vol. 1, 2). Generals Grant and Banks reviewed the entire 13th Army Corps on September 5. Grant supposedly noticed the fine performance of the 11th Indiana at this event. A few days later, Banks invited the regiment to perform a dress parade in Coliseum Square, an event that drew one of the largest crowds in New Orleans to see a dress parade for a single regiment. Banks and Thomas attended and complimented the Hoosiers, and the *New Orleans Delta* labeled the 11th "one of the most celebrated regiments of Western troops" whose deeds were familiar to all, and noted the regiment's careful instruction made them quite proficient in the manual of arms (*Indianapolis Daily Journal*, 25 September 1863).

worsted them on every part of the ground. They were anxious to get the better of us in some way so they boasted that Colonel Purlee [sic] of New York had a horse that could beat, on a mile race, any horse the Western boys had and to show that they meant just what they said, they proposed to bet two to one on the Colonel's horse.[146] General Hovey's orderly had picked up a little gray mare in Mississippi on the Vicksburg campaign and we thought she could run so we found out the time of their horse and without their knowledge or consent, we put the little gray on the track and timed her and found she could beat their horse. We arranged for the race and proceeded to take their bets. But we were up against a proposition when we found out that Colonel Purdee [sic] would allow no one but himself to ride his horse and he would ride against noone [sic] but a commissioned officer. We were up against the real thing when we had no officer who was an expert rider that was not too heavy for the little gray to carry, but we could not think of being beaten or have to strike our colors, so we found a little fellow in our regiment that had been a professional jockey. We took him down in the city and had a full officers dress suit made for him and put captain's shoulder straps on him. When the race was ready to be run, we introduced our private in captain's uniform as "Captain so-and-so" to Colonel Purlee, which was very satisfactory to the Colonel's dignity. Of course the little gray won the

[145] The Seventh Regiment, New York State Militia was perhaps the most famous state militia unit in existence when the Civil War began. The well trained and equipped regiment left New York City to defend Washington in April 1861, and garrisoned Baltimore in 1862 and 1863, but saw no combat during the war (Michael J. McAfee, "Uniforms and History: The Seventh Regiment New York State Militia," *Military Images* 13/5 [March–April 1992]: 30–31; David O'Reilly, "The Dandy 7th," *Military Images* 20/5 [March–April 1999]: 32–37).

[146] Forty-two-year-old Samuel R. Per Lee was colonel of the 114th New York Infantry, a part of Major General William B. Franklin's 19th Army Corps in the summer of 1863 (US War Department, *The War of the Rebellion: A Compilation of the Official Records of the Union and Confederate Armies* [Washington, DC: Government Printing Office, 1880–1901] ser. 1, vol. 26, pt. 1, pp. 710–11; New York Adjutant General, *Annual Report of the Adjutant-General of the State of New York for the Year 1903*, serial 35 [Albany: Oliver A. Quayle, 1904] 94).

race and the money was transferred from the Eastern to the Western boys. The Eastern boys were sore but game, they wanted to get their money back and were willing to take another chance at the Western wheel of fortune.

They brought out a little sorrel mare built like a greyhound and looked like she could almost fly. They proposed backing her against anything we had on a quarter mile race. I was appointed a committee of one to find a horse among the Western boys that could beat her. A fellow in the 21st Indiana regiment showed me a great old lumox of a horse that had every appearance of being an old dray horse. He swore the old horse could beat the little sorrel—that he had beaten everything in Southern Indiana on a quarter mile race. I told him I did not believe his old "winding blades" of a horse could run fast as a cow and that the little sorrel would go out under the wire before he could get the old steamboat started. But he still contended his old horse could beat the little sorrel and proposed putting up his last dollar and the horse with it that he could win. I then told him as I was unable to see his horse's running qualities I would have to take his word but that I would have to bet on his word instead of the horse. I knew if the old horse could run anything like the fellow represented we would have a dead cinch on the Eastern boys, for I knew as soon as they saw the old horse that they would put up their last dollar on the little sorrel. So when we trotted the old horse out they went wild. They not only put up every dollar they had but put up their valuables, watches, etc. They bet three to one and some bet five to one. Our boys accommodated them by taking all their bets but we did this on a bluff rather than strike our colors. We had no faith in the old horse winning for the little sorrel was a beauty and a trained quarter racer. But to our great astonishment and delight, the "old winding blades" ran right off from the little sorrel, so again money was transferred from East to West.

The Eastern boys had their nerve right with them, and as a final test challenged our boys to a game of poker—that innocent game of cards that soldiers sometimes indulged in as a preventative of homesickness. They were cleaned up at that; in fact, we cleaned them up and beat them on every part of the ground and they soon learned to respect us and took great pleasure in giving us the military salute when they met us.

About the middle of September, 1863, we started on an expedition up in the Tuckapa country in Southwest Louisiana with the purpose of driving the rebel General Dick Taylor back into Texas. General Franklin was in command of the expedition. We crossed the river from New Orleans to Algers, [sic] took a railroad train there for Brasier [sic] City, which is located on Burwick Bay about two miles from the Gulf of Mexico. Here was our first sight of salt water. As soon as we were halted we all doffed our clothes for a good swim in salt water. Some of the boys were far out in the bay when a large school of porpoises came in sight. Their bodies looked to be about the size of a horse. As they rose to the top of the water for air they looked as though they were turning somersaults. As none of us had ever seen such monsters before but had read much about sharks, we lost no time in getting the idea in our minds that these fearful looking creatures of the sea were sharks and as they were headed right toward us we took it for granted they were hungry for meat and had sighted a harvest. It looked as though they were trying to beat each other to us. When we first saw them several fellows yelled "sharks" and this caused a stampede. There were several hundred of us quite a distance from shore and our frantic efforts to get to shore was one of the most ridiculous sights I have ever witnessed. I have seen stampedes on land but this stampede in water capped them all, the pawing, and kicking of air and water, the scramble to get ahead, knowing the hindmost fellow would be the first sweet food for the sharks. The grandeur of this stampede was beyond description but our fright did not destroy our bravery for as soon as we got to our guns on shore we opened a murderous fire on the beasts. We were disappointed when we found out they were such innocent critters.

We remained in camp on the shore of the bay for a few days and had a fine time eating oysters and catching crabs. I was very shy of swimming in the bayous as they were full of alligators. I saw one take a negro under one day and after that I felt like I never needed a bath in a bayou. The morning of October 3 we crossed Burwick Bay and marched in the direction of Franklin. We reached Franklin on the 4th and left the morning of the 5th.

I was not well, the weather was extremely hot and on the march that day about 11:00 o'clock [sic] a.m., I was overcome by the heat and had my first sunstroke. I fell and was picked up and thrown in an ambulance. I was unconscious. A soon as we went into bivouac for the night, some of the boys of the company worked with me and I returned to consciousness some time in the night. The next morning Colonel McCauley [sic] put me on his horse. It required a great effort to keep in the saddle but I managed to do so, for our ambulances were full. The extreme heat caused many of the soldiers to get sick.

On the 6th we marched 12 miles and bivouacked within two miles of New Iber[i]a. We remained there until the morning of the 10th. I had so recovered in the meantime that I was able to march, yet I was quite weak from the effects of my sunstroke and after marching 25 miles that day in the hot sun I felt that I was about ready for the "cooling board." I felt all day that it would be a great relief if I could drop dead but I had my nerve with me and followed the flag until we went into bivouac that night on the banks of Vermillion Bayou. On the 15th of October we received orders and started on a forced march at 5:00 p.m. to support the 19th army corps. We marched 21 miles from 5:00 p.m. until midnight when we reached the camp of the 19th corps. On the morning of the 16th we were in line of battle. The enemy made a dash on our cavalry but we drove them back.[147]

On the 21st we marched 15 miles, skirmishing and driving the enemy before us all day. We passed through the town of Appolusus. I was on the skirmish line all day. We bivouacked for the night at Barr's Landing on Corcaublau Bayou. This is about 12 miles Northwest of Appolusus, Louisiana.[148] On October 29th we started on our return march to New Orleans. The enemy followed us and we were in a constant skirmish with them. They picked up many of our stragglers. On the night of the 2nd of November six of the 2nd Louisiana cavalry deserted and went to the enemy and informed them of our position and on the morning of the 3rd the enemy attacked General Burbridge's brigade. Burbridge only had about 1100 men and the enemy attacked with 8000 of which about half were mounted. They took about 500 of Burbridge's men prisoner before our division could get up to his relief. It was not long after we got into the fight until the enemy retreated. In this fight we lost 20 killed and 100 wounded. The loss of the enemy was much greater besides the 100 prisoners we took.[149]

When we reached New Iber[i]a my company was sent out the night of the 19th of November on a scout to Spanish Lake, some seven miles from New Iber[i]a.[150] We were informed there was a

---

[147] The itinerary of the 1st Brigade, 3rd Division, 13th Corps reads, "Marched to Buzzard Prairie; enemy drove in our grand guard, but would not attack" (*Official Records*, ser. 1, vol. 26, pt. 1, p. 367).

[148] The itinerary of the 1st Brigade for 21 October reported the brigade "Left Buzzard Prairie; skirmished with the enemy and drove them through Opelousas, La., and encamped at Barre's Landing, 8 miles beyond the latter place" (ibid.).

[149] Beginning 3 October 1863, General Nathaniel P. Banks led a column up the Bayou Teche, intending to turn west at present-day Lafayette LA and move into Texas. Eventually Banks turned over command to General William B. Franklin, who led the force as far as Opelousas. Faced with a lack of water and subsistence along the route, the Federals retreated to New Iberia LA by mid-November. During the retreat, on 3 November 1863, near Grand Coteau, a Federal brigade of Stephen G. Burbridge's Division was attacked, and 200 members of the 67th Indiana Regiment were captured. The arrival of the 11th Indiana and other Federal forces forced the Confederates to withdraw (Welcher, *Union Army*, vol. 2, 56–57, 264–65).

camp of rebels there and we were ordered to break up the camp. Just at daybreak on the morning of the 20th we surprised the camp and captured twelve officers and 98 men. They belonged to the 7th Texas cavalry. We killed and wounded several but we had no loss.[151]

We arrived at Algiers, a town just across the Mississippi River from New Orleans, during the night of December 22, 1863. In this campaign into Southwest Louisiana we suffered much from the extreme heat in the early part of the campaign, also from want of water which was fit to drink. Much of the time the only water we could get was in sloughs covered with a heavy green scum and so warm and muddy that it was sickening and caused many of our soldiers to die of fever. Most of the country we passed through was beautiful to look at and was mostly prairie. The Bayous, as they are called, were more like sluggish or dead-water rivers. All were alive with alligators. There is a skirt of timber all along these bayous, mostly live oak and the trees are covered with Spanish moss which hangs clear to the ground. When the wind is blowing and this moss is waving to and fro it is a beautiful sight. I saw a few large sugar plantations with vats filled with thousands of barrels of Orleans molasses. All the people, both white and black, in Southwestern Louisiana spoke French and very few could understand English. All the able bodied negroes were gone from the plantations, some had enlisted in the Union army, others had been put in the rebel army by their masters and were building fortifications, but we found hundreds of negro women and children on these plan[t]ations.

---

[150] The 1st Brigade, 3rd Division, 13th Corps moved to New Iberia on 17 November 1863 (*Official Records,* ser. 1, vol. 26, pt. 1, p.367).

[151] In conjunction with some Union cavalrymen, the 11th Indiana participated in a 20 November attack on Camp Pratt LA, an outpost of 120 men belonging to the 7th Texas Cavalry. There is some disagreement as to the number of Confederate losses. According to the itinerary of the 1st Brigade, 3rd Division, 13th Army Corps, thirteen Confederate officers and ninety-eight enlisted men were captured. Union Brigadier General Albert L. Lee's report states 12 officers and 101 enlisted men were taken, with 1 rebel killed, and 3 wounded (ibid., 367, 369–70, 378).

A Yankee army was a great sight to them and caused a great deal of excitement among them. They would all come out and stand by the road and watch us march by. For the sake of a little amusement I would grab a little kid up in my arms and walk off with it. It was fun to see how excited these old aunties would get and hear them jabber French. Finally a hundred or more of them would form themselves into a rescue party and take after me. Then I would drop the kid and step into ranks where they could not tell me from the other soldiers and none of the boys would give me away. Such little innocent sport as this was a great treat to the soldiers and caused them to forget how tired and sick they were. One day I was in command of the skirmish line. I was three or four hundred yards in advance of the line of battle when I came to some negro quarters. I stopped to ask the negroes some questions in regard to the enemy as I knew they had passed there ahead of me. A large crowd of old fat bench-legged aunties gathered around me, most of them with their arms full of little pick-aninnies, all gabbing and jabbering at the same time, greatly excited. There was a strip of timber right ahead of me where I expected the enemy to make a stand. I looked back and saw our battery in position, ready to shell the woods in front of me. I knew the shells would pass close over our heads and I could not keep from laughing in anticipation of the consternation there would be among these old aunties when the shells came whistling and shrieking over their heads. I was not disappointed, for the first volley that passed over our heads caused them all to drop flat on the ground as though they had been shot through. They lay there, most of them on top of the children they had held in their arms, with no effort to get up, notwithstanding the little ones under them who were kicking and squalling—at least all of those who were not being smothered. After a while one old aunty rolled the whites of her eyes up at me and said,

"De Lord God, Mass Yank, ain't you fraid dem dar tings will kill you?"
This was a very amusing sight to me.

One day on this campaign I was put in command of a detail of
soldiers to go out and feel for the enemy and locate him if possible. I
came to a field. There was a house at the far end of the field and a
lane on the left side and to the left of the house a ravine ran from in
front of the house back through the field, causing the field to run to a
point at the house. There was timber in the ravine beyond the house.
I made up my mind that the enemy was in this timber. I told the boys
if the rebels were in that timber I would play a Yank trick on them. I
placed some of my men behind the fence near the head of the ravine
and placed the others in the fence corners near the mouth of the lane.
I told the boys I was going to walk toward the house about equal
distance from the ravine and lane, that if the rebels were in the timber
as I thought they were, they would see me in the field alone and
would send a squad of cavalry up the ravine and another up the lane
to surround and capture me and as soon as I saw them I would run
back just fast enough to force them to make their circle near the fence
where they were secreted and for them to wait until the rebels got in
close range and then open fire on them and dismount as many as
possible. My ruse worked like a charm. The boys knocked several out
of their saddles, the others retreated as fast as their horses could carry
them and we gave a yell that made them think a whole army was after
them. Those rebels thought they had a dead sure thing on the capture
of a Yank officer. I hated to disappoint them but everything is
supposed to be fair in war.

Most of the time on this campaign we were very short of rations.
On our return march we were out of meat for quite a while and
General Franklin one day sent a detail of cavalry out to forage for
cattle. They returned with several hundred head of sheep and cattle
and were driving them past our camp, taking them on ahead to the

General's headquarters, when a cow that was on the warpath dashed into our company quarters and made a vicious charge on a bunch of our boys who were standing in the camp street. Joe Hanna dodged her and grabbed her by the tail as she tried to turn on him. The other boys tackled her and it was not a minute until they had her slaughtered. About this time the boys of the regiment saw the drove of sheep and made a grand charge on them. I do not think it was more than three minutes from the time the first sheep was on the shoulder of a soldier until the last one was butchered and the men were making for camp with their loads. Our regiment got all the sheep. As the herd was driven past other camps the soldiers would rush into the herd, grab a calf by the tail and drag it off to their quarters. It was amusing to see a soldier grab a two-year-old by the tail and swing on his tailhold until the brute got too swift for him, his feet would fly out and up and his head strike the ground and his tailhold would slip.

That night Colonel Macauley received an order from General Franklin to have his regiment searched and to have every sheep he could find which had not been butchered, driven to his headquarters next morning, and to arrest every man in his regiment found with either a sheep or fresh meat and send them to him for punishment. It was dark when the Colonel received this order and he sent for all the officers of the regiment to report at once to his headquarters. When we had all reported, he instructed us to tell all the soldiers of our companies that he would have the regiment searched the next morning and every one found with fresh meat or a sheep in his tent would be arrested and turned over to the General. When we notified the boys of what was to be done it was hint enough, for three years' experience in the army had educated them to all the tricks of the trade. They knew it meant "hide your meat before morning." When the search was made in the morning there was not so much as a bunch of wool that could be found in camp to indicate there had ever been a sheep there, except one very old and very poor sheep that the Colonel found tied to his tent when he got up that morning. The Colonel acknowledged the joke in the best of humor.

When we got back to Algiers it was the winter season for that country and we were having cold rains every day which made it very disagreeable. Not being able to write while on the march I was behind with my company records. In order to be more comfortable while writing, I built a chimney and fireplace in my tent. I was the only officer in the regiment who had a fire and a comfortable tent. January 1, 1864—the day known all over this country by those who were living then, as the cold New Year of 1864, I was sitting at my stand writing up my records when a gang of officers crowded into my tent. It rather vexed me as I was anxious to get my records brought up to date. I gave up my seat and stepped outside my tent to cool off a little. As the Dutch Quartermaster, who had insulted me at Dawson's Plantation when I was Orderly Sergeant, was with the officers in my tent (we had never been on visiting terms), I knew his only object in coming was to enjoy the comforts of my fire and not my society and it made me angry. When I re-entered the tent this quartermaster, thinking to be cute in the presence of the other officers, grabbed my beard as I entered and gave it a jerk. That opened up business at once. All the wrath I had been smothering for nearly a year flashed to the surface and I downed him and was choking him before he could realize what was transpiring. He offered no resistance. I let him up and as soon as he got to his feet he reached for my big wooden inkstand and hurled it at my head, grazing my temple and burning it sufficiently to fire my temper again. I dealt him a fearful blow on the temple with my fist and he dropped as if he had been shot. I then proceeded to put a head and face on him that would do to wear in good society. While giving his face some extra touches I reminded him of the insult he had given me almost a year before, when it would have been a high crime for me to have struck him. I told him this was simply settlement for the insult. The officers tried to pull me off but I had a good grip on his collar. They pulled me out of the tent but I held onto my man, dragging him with me and dealing him blows until I felt the debt was settled in full. As soon as I had finished this very pleasant task to my own satisfaction, the boys of my company hiked me onto their shoulders and marched through camp with a great hurrah. They did not like the Dutchman and had been wanting to see him licked for a long while. It cured him of his abusive and overbearing manner and we became good friends after this little settlement of accounts.

The smallpox broke out in camp here and several of our soldiers died of the disease. This was one of the worst camps we had ever had. The ground was low and flat and as it was raining nearly every day, cold and disagreeable and the mud deep, it made it an unhealthy and undesirable camp. On the 19th of January 1864 we broke camp, crossed the river to New Orleans, thence to Lake Pouchartrain [sic] and there we boarded a boat, crossed the lake, which is about 25 miles wide, and went about three miles up the Chufuncta River to a little town called Madisonville. Here we disembarked and went into camp. However, I did not disembark with the regiment.

I was placed in command of the boat with a battalion of about three hundred men and ordered to run the boat up the river and ascertain if there was a body of the enemy camped near the river. I went some 50 or 75 miles up the river but found no camp of the enemy. I found a few bushwhackers along the banks. At this time Colonel Macauley was in command of the brigade and Major George M. Butler was in command of the regiment. Butler was a little "cock-robin" of a fellow and there was little friendship between us.[152] He was pompous and overbearing. The boys of the regiment did not like him. When I returned from my expedition up the river I found an order from Butler in my tent, relieving me of the command of my company and placing Copeland, a lieutenant of his old company, in command of my company.[153] The order gave no reason for relieving me. I knew Copeland was a pet of his and I took it for granted that it was just an effort on the part of Major Butler to help Copeland to promotion. The Major and I came near having some serious trouble the next morning when he came into my tent and gave me some orders in regard to the company. I informed him that under his order I was not in command of the company and suggested that if he had orders to give in regard to the company that he had better give them to the officer he had placed in command of the company. He wanted to know if I did not propose to help command it. I told him that so long as I stood relieved of the command I did not propose to command it. He then informed me that if I did not propose to help command it I could get out of the company. At this I reached for my Navy and told him he could get out of my tent if he would be real quick about it. He got—and that closed the conversation but I felt sure I was booked for a courtmartial. Colonel Macauley came to see me the same day of this trouble and assured me he would see to it that no trouble would come to me for "hiking" the Major out of my tent. As soon as Colonel Macauley returned to the regiment which was but two or three days after this trouble, he issued an order relieving Copeland of command and placing me back in command of my company. This difficulty with Major Butler and the one I had

---

[152] George Butler of Indianapolis entered the army in April 1861 as a first lieutenant in Company A, 11th Indiana (three months). He then became the captain of Company A in the three years' regiment before being promoted to major in March 1863. No doubt much to Durham's displeasure, Butler served as major until he was mustered out in July 1865 (William H. H. Terrell, *Report of the Adjutant General of the State of Indiana*, vol. 2 [Indianapolis: W. R. Holloway, 1865] 28, 75, 77).

[153] Benjamin F. Copeland of Indianapolis was commissioned a second lieutenant of Company A, 11th Indiana in October 1862, a first lieutenant in March 1863, and was mustered out in December 1864 (Terrell, *Report of the Adjutant General*, vol. 2, 77).

with the Dutchman was all the trouble I had during the war with the officers.

We had a beautiful camp here in Madisonville on the edge of a dense pine forest. There is a very large scope of country here covered with a very heavy growth of pine and is known by the natives as the "Piney Woods." There were hundreds of people of all nationalities in this pine forest, making turpentine and tar. Few of them had ever been outside of the woods. They were extremely ignorant and not half clad. I saw women with nothing but an old greasy homespun cotton skirt on with which to hide their nakedness but they did not seem to realize that they were not properly clad. I found men in that pinery who honestly believed they had voted for old Andrew Jackson at the last presidential election. They had all heard of the battle General Jackson fought at New Orleans and of course his name was revered by everyone in that country. As none of these people could read, all a politician had to do was furnish them with tickets and tell them General Jackson was the candidate and they would vote it solid. I was amused at an old Irishman I met in these woods one day. I asked him who he voted for in the last election for President and with great pride he said "And be Jases I voted for General Jackson. I have voted for him all my life and expect to as long as I live for he is the greatest mon that ever lived." The old fellow got fighting mad when I told him Jackson had been dead for many years but he considered it a Yankee lie and doubtless continued to vote for Jackson to the end of his life.

We had more real enjoyment at this camp than at any other camp we had during the war. Our orders were not strict, for there was no enemy near and we had no place to go except in the Piney Woods. Our principal sport was swinging. There were some old abandoned boats at the landing where we could get ropes for our swings. We made one boss swing. We trimmed the limbs off a couple of tall pine trees that stood about ten feet apart. We fastened our ropes to the top of these trees more than a hundred feet from the ground. We made a seat large enough for two men to sit side by side and we had a small rope about 200 feet long that we ran through a ring and one man in the swing would hold the end of this rope where he gripped the swing. A dozen or more soldiers would take the other end of the small rope and run with all their speed. If the man in the swing should let go this rope at the right time it would send him higher than the top of the trees, giving him a sweep over 300 feet. Very few could stand this full sweep as in making the descent from the highest point the swing would reach more than one hundred feet. One could not breathe. I made many full sweeps on this swing and somehow the danger was fascinating to me. It was great sport for the daredevil boys to get a tenderfoot in and give him a good sweep. One day I got the assistant surgeon to get in the swing with me. I knew he was a very cowardly man about taking such chances. We made him believe we would just give him a little swing but it was our intention to give him a full sweep and it was the greatest sweep ever made on the swing. It sent us about 50 feet above the top of the trees. I thought it was going full circle and the surgeon became so frightened he was limp as a rag. I had to hold him in the swing as he had let all holds loose. I thought I would have to let him fall in spite of all I could do and came near losing my own hold several times in my efforts to hold him. There was no such thing as stopping the swing until it ran down. Had I got the least bit rattled we would have both been dashed to death but it took all my strength and wits to hold him in and keep from falling myself. It was the last time I introduced a tenderfoot to a full sweep.

While at this camp we had a little sport at the expense of our Chaplain. One of the duties of the chaplain was to look after the mail for the regiment. In the fall of 1863 when it was learned we were going to have a very long and arduous campaign in Southwest

Louisiana, the chaplain, in order to get out of this campaign, got himself detailed at Memphis, Tenn. He had been absent from the regiment for several months and the whole regiment was tired of his neglect of duty. Colonel Macauley sent him an order to return to the regiment at once or he would have him dishonorably discharged from the service. This order scared the chaplain and he returned at once and to make fair weather with the officers he brought a five gallon demijohn of whiskey. But the parson made a great mistake. Instead of setting his demijohn out and saying, "Come boys, all of you and drink of my spirits, it is my treat and drink hearty," he tried to sell it to the officers by the drink—proper saloon fashion. We did not take well to that kind of treat. I thought I could make an amendment to it so I watched to see where he deposited his demijohn for safekeeping that night. I found he put it in the hospital tent or rather the tent where the hospital supplies were kept. There was always a guard placed at this tent but I saw it was a Company F man on guard that night so I went to Lieutenant Pansey [sic] of this company and got him to go and tell the guard that he and I were going to have a little game of cards that night in his tent and for the guard to bring us a drink from the parson's demijohn at 10 o'clock.[154] I then notified two other officers to be on the watch for the guard to leave the tent and when he did for them to swipe the demijohn. So the guard brought us the refreshments and the parson's demijohn was soon in our possession. Every night for a week after that the officers of the regiment would get together and hold a "pow wow" and about mightnight [sic] after taking freely of our refreshments we would go in a body to the chaplain's tent and serenade him. But he was smart enough to take it all in good humor.

---

[154] Louis Panse of Cumberland IN was commissioned a second lieutenant in Company F of the 11th in March 1863 and a first lieutenant in Company H in November of the same year. Transferred back to Company F, Panse served until mustered out in December 1864 (Terrell, *Report of the Adjutant General*, vol. 2, 80, 82).

Chapter 9

NEW YORK AND HOME

Our three years' enlistment was now drawing to a close. We commenced re-enlisting the men of the regiment for veteran service, which meant for the duration of the war. By the 24th of February most all the men of the regiment had re-enlisted.[155] We broke camp on the 24th and crossed the Lake to New Orleans and went into camp. We at once applied to General Banks for transportation home by way of New York, which he granted. We then sent a challenge to the New York 7th regiment for a competitive drill, instructing them to name the amount of money we would drill for and we would cover it.

While in camp here the officers of the regiment took all the men who had re-enlisted to the St. Charles Theater to see The Cricket, played by Emma Madred as Cricket. Three evenings afterward the theater management gave the regiment complimentary tickets. On March 4, 1864 we boarded the steamer Charles Thomas at New Orleans for New York. We had high seas most of the way to Key West. We reached Key West the 9th but as we had a case of smallpox on our ship we were not allowed to land for coal. The fellow with smallpox lay right at my stateroom door so in passing in and out of my room I

---

[155] In 1863, the US Adjutant General's Office granted furloughs of thirty days to men who reenlisted "for three years or during the war," before their current terms expired. In addition, if three-fourths of the soldiers in a regiment rejoined, they could travel home as a unit. Troops who reenlisted also got free transportation home, a $402 bounty, and the right to be referred to as "Veteran Volunteers." A total of 296 men of the 11th Indiana reenlisted as veterans (US War Department, *The War of the Rebellion: A Compilation of the Official Records of the Union and Confederate Armies* [Washington, DC: Government Printing Office, 1880–1901] ser. 3, vol. 3, pp. 414–16, 1084, 1179; William H. H. Terrell, *Report of the Adjutant General of the State of Indiana*, vol. 1 [Indianapolis: Alexander H. Conner, 1869] 8.

had to pass within a foot of his head. It made me feel a little nervous. But the smallpox patient was finally taken off the ship and we were allowed to land. We marched through the town, our band playing and it looked as though nearly everyone in town was following us. It was the most motley outfit one could imagine. They were of all nationalities. Most all the young girls and many of the boys were perfectly nude while the grown ones wore nothing but a homespun cotton slip. We halted in the street to give them a little drill and while we were drilling this crowd that had followed us got to fighting among themselves and it was an amusing fight. Every nationality had his own peculiar method or style of fighting. The Irish used their shillelagh, Spaniards and Mexicans with their stilettos, others would stand up and knock like Americans, while the negroes would butt, bite and gnaw like dogs. It assumed the proportions of a riot.

We remained at Key West all day and night. In the afternoon I was strolling along the beach gathering shells and watching pelicans light on the water when I decided to take a swim. I swam far out from the shore; then the idea struck me that I was liable to be taken under by a shark as I had seen many of them following our ship, so I about-faced for shore and the more I thought of sharks the worse scared I got. I looked over my shoulder once to see if there was any sea monster after me. As I turned my head my beard floated over my shoulder and I got a glimpse of it and thought sure a shark was right on me. I made a lunge that sent me clear out of the water—almost. There was no one there to time me so I have no record of my speed in making shore but I am satisfied it was a record breaker. When I got back to the ship I learned that a fellow had just been taken under by the sharks and I could see hundreds of them swimming around the ship seeking someone to devour. When I saw this I felt that I had made a narrow escape. I want to say right here I do not like the countenance of a shark, nor do I like the expression of his eyes.

While we had high seas from Key West to New York, especially as we rounded Cape Hatteras, yet we had a jolly good time. We formed what we called the "Hoo Doo Club" and this would meet every day and night in the smoking room. The entertainments generally consisted of smoking, singing, recitations and story telling. We arrived in New York City on March 17th. The old New York 7th regiment met us but did not accept our challenge for a competitive drill. We gave a parade drill in City Hall Park and the 7th was out in a body to see us drill. They acknowledged that we could beat them.[156] While there I dined at the Astor House at three fifty per "dine." I visited Central Park, Barnum's Museum and Theater, etc. The old 7th entertained us royally, paying all our expenses.

From the time I was a lad up until the war my father took the New York Tribune and there was always one page of it devoted to accounts of the confidence games played by the New York sharpers and the cappers for the gambling dens of the city, how they would take the unsophisticated stranger in and rob him, etc. My father would always read these accounts to me and wind up by telling me that when my time came to get out into the world I would be the first sucker the sharpers would get. It always made me mad as a hornet when my father would tell me this. I could not see why he thought I would be such an easy subject for a sharper to work on. I thought my father was gauging my ability away below par. I did not see his object but later on I realized the fact that his object was to post me on their tricks so that I would know a sharper when I met him. When I did get out into the world I felt very thankful to my father for doing that

---

[156] The 11th Indiana arrived in New York on 17 March 1864, and held a dress parade the following day "by request of friends who consider them the best drilled regiment in the service." Thousands gathered to witness the dress parade and bayonet exercises, and the *New York Times* admitted that the performance of the Hoosiers "went far toward justifying the claim" that they were the best drilled in the army. The men of the 11th enjoyed applause and the "heartiest cheers" from the crowd (*New York Times*, 18 March, 19 March 1864).

which formerly made me so angry. It saved me of having to learn these things in the great school of experience, for soon after I landed in New York City I was down on Broadway making some purchases and a very smooth looking gentleman followed me into the store.

My first glance at the man satisfied me that he was one of those sharpers my father had read to me so much about when I was a lad. I at once made up my mind to play the sucker. He rushed up to me and gave me a most hearty greeting, calling me captain — (somebody). It was more than a minute before he discovered that I was not really his old friend. He finally discovered his mistake but I looked so much like him he could not help having a friendly feeling toward me. He kindly assisted me in making my purchases. He asked me where I was from and I told him I was from "Injiany" and he also was from Indiana and was a quartermaster on leave of absence from the Potomac Army. In a moment a friend stepped in and he introduced his friend as Doctor —, a surgeon in the army and also from Indiana and both were on their way back to the army. They doubtless took me as belonging to a new regiment that was on its way to the front.

After finishing my purchases we stepped out on the sidewalk and my friend asked me which way I was going. I told him. He said he was going the same way and if I did not care he would walk with me. Of course I expressed pleasure to have his company. He then asked the doctor if he would walk with us. He accepted the invitation and as soon as we started up the street my friend very cautiously asked me if I ever "imbibed." I pretended I did not know what he meant and he explained to me that he wished to know whether I ever drank anything. When I finally seemed to "catch on," I told him with an embarrassed grin that I had drunk a little wine with the boys two or three times since I left home. He told me he knew of a little place in the city to get a drink and we would go there. I had made up my mind I would go with them to their den. I was wearing my sword and side arms and I knew I was above the average as an athlete and felt sure if it should come to a showdown I could get as many of them as they could of me. I felt satisfied that if I did not take their bait I could get out without a racket, but was equally sure if I took their bait and then jumped the game I would have to fight my way out.

When we got to my friend's fine drinking place we climbed several flights of stairs and turned into a room where there was a bar in front of the door. The moment I stepped in I saw it was a gambling den. I saw fellows at the back end of the hall playing faro. When we stepped up to the bar my friend asked me what I would take. With a silly grin I asked him what he was going to take. He would take a little whiskey, so I guessed I would take some of the same. My object in this was to impress him with my greenness and to make sure they could not dope me as in this case my friend and I would both drink from the same bottle. After we drank my friend was astonished to find the doctor did not drink with us. He finally discovered him at the back end of the hall sitting at the fero [sic] table. My friend suggested that we go back and see what the doctor was doing. We found the doctor raking in greenbacks by the handsful. I stood with eyes and mouth open with supposed surprise and astonishment. All this time my friend was nudging me and saying the doctor is doing pretty well. When sufficiently recovered from my astonishment to speak I asked my friend what he called that. He said that it was faro and proceeded to tell me how I could win every time (sometimes). He assured me he could beat the game on every part of the ground and insisted on me sitting down with him and he would show me how I could win a pile of money; but I still looked on with eyes and mouth open and told him I could not just understand yet how it was done. He continued to explain while the doctor, as an object lesson, continued to rake in the money.

After I had fooled with my friend long as I thought I dared, without him suspecting me, I turned to him with a friendly smile and told him he was a pretty good capper but that I could give him a pointer that would help him in his business. I told him whe[ne]ver he undertook to cap a soldier hereafter to let his first question be, "How long have you been in the army?" I said "If he has been in two or three years, be a little careful for he is liable to know as much about the game as you do, and this precaution may save you embarrassment." I told him I had not time now to buck the tiger but I had some friends who were pretty good at the game and if he would kindly give me his card we would perhaps call later and give his tiger a whirl. The joke was decidedly on my friend and the other fellows threw down their cards and were convulsed with laughter. They collared my friend and marched him to the bar and made him set them up to the crowd. I cost him about ten dollars to cap me. So, as my father used to tell me, they spotted me for a sucker and I let them take me to their den but they did not "do me."

We left the city of New York the night of the 18th and arrived at the city of Buffalo about midnight the night of the 19th. As Colonel Macauley was a native of Buffalo, the citizens met us at the depot, took us to a hall where they had a banquet prepared for us. The whole regiment was seated at one table. They gave us the freedom of the city but I was almost chilled to death. When we left the Gulf the temperature ranged from 90 to 98 and here there was snow and ice five or six feet thick with a cold wind blowing from the lake. We left Buffalo the night of the 20th and arrived at Indianapolis the 22nd. Here we were feasted and toasted for three days and I arrived home the night of March 26, 1864.[157]

---

[157] Lengthy descriptions of the 11th Indiana's arrival in Indianapolis and the subsequent dinner may be found in the *Indianapolis Daily Journal*, 23 March, 24 March 1864.

Chapter 10

COPPERHEADS AND THE END OF SERVICE

I immediately went to work recruiting for the veteran service. When I got home I found the "Knights of the Golden Circle" (which meant Northern rebels) were growing very impudent.[158] They guarded the crossings on Rock River or Sugar Creek as it was called. This was a large stream about three miles North of my home. There was a large settlement of the rebels on the North side of the river and if there was a Union man in the whole outfit he dared not acknowledge it. These Northern rebels or copperheads as we called them, were harboring "bounty jumpers" and deserters from the army, burning houses of Union men and committing all kinds of depredations. They had regular military companies formed and drilled them. They had repulsed our home guard or state militia company, when they attempted to cross the river to search for deserters.[159]

The April election was held about two weeks after I got home and I went to our town, Waveland, to vote. There I met a lot of young fellows who had never gone into the army but whom I thought could have gone in with less sacrifice than I had made, therefore, I had little respect for them. They told me about how the copperheads had licked our home guards and how the guards were afraid to cross the

---

[158] The Knights of the Golden Circle was a secret, pre-Civil War Southern organization dedicated to secession. Reputedly the organization spread into Northern states as well once the war began, including Indiana. The group was said to have held secret meetings to organize activities to disrupt the Union war effort and aid the Confederacy, such as encouraging desertions and hiding men who had been drafted. At least some Midwestern anti-administration "Copperheads," or Northern Peace Democrats, had ties to the KGC (Patricia L. Faust, ed., *Historical Times Illustrated Encyclopedia of the Civil War* [New York: Harper Collins Publishers, 1986] 420, 564). A lengthy discussion of the KGC may be found in G. R. Tredway, *Democratic Opposition to the Lincoln Administration in Indiana* (Indianapolis: Indiana Historical Bureau, 1973) 108–35.

river, etc. I told them that if twelve of them would volunteer to follow me I would assure them I would take them across the river. Some of them agreed to go with me. I then went to work raising my squad for the raid and just here I wish to give a little side incident.

I was very busy and greatly interested in raising my squad. I had provided myself with a cigar and was puffing some like a six horse-power engine, when in turning the corner of a street I met my father face to face. We both halted as I had no chance to hide my cigar. As the Texan said, "It was a far sqar cotch." My father stood and looked at me for more than a minute—neither spoke. I saw the tears come in his eyes and he finally said, "My son, if you give down at one point you will give down at another. I would be a man and stand on the square." He had given me many hard thrashings but never in my life had he given me one that hurt and pained me as this did. I saw how it really hurt him. Had he scolded me I would not have cared but the hurt I saw it gave him to see that I had fallen from his teachings was painful to me and how true, I afterwards found, were his words when he said, "if you give down at one point you will at another." While I did not quit smoking, I never let him see me use tobacco after that.

I finally got my squad of braves together. They were armed with all kinds of guns and revolvers that would make a noise. I was determined if we met any resistance to lead them into the thickest and hottest part of it. I was anxious for them to get a sniff of rebel

---

[159] The pro-Union *Parke County* (IN) *Republican* reported a number of disturbances between "Copperheads" and Unionists during the war. Sugar Creek Township in Parke County (just west of Durham's hometown of Waveland) was noted for such incidents. Examples may be found in the 11 November and 9 December 1863 and 13 January 1864 issues. Likewise, many years after the war, a history of Montgomery County noted that in Ripley Township, just north of where Durham lived, there was Democratic resistance to the township officer charged with enrolling men for the draft. The unpopular officer was ordered to leave the county, and when he refused, several hundred Democrats organized to make sure he complied. The county sheriff arrested six of the group's leaders, but when the Democrats threatened to march on Crawfordsville to free their friends, the men were released and a new enrolling officer was appointed (A. W. Bowen and Co., *History of Montgomery County Indiana*, vol. 1 [Indianapolis: A. W. Bowen and Co., 1913] 178–79).

powder. I knew when it came to a showdown these copperheads were cowards and all a fellow had to do was go at them like he was killing copperhead snakes and they would stampede. About night I started with my mounted battalion of heroes for the seat of war. I met with no resistance in crossing the river. I had the names of all the leading copperheads in that section of the country.

The first house I came to that I wanted to search, I threw the guards around the house, then I went to the door and demanded admission. Through a window I could see the man getting his gun. I told him I had his house surrounded and for him to attempt to shoot only meant his certain death. He opened the door and I searched his house and then made him go with me and pilot me to the next house I wished to search. When we got near the house I turned our pilot loose and ordered him home. I then made this man pilot me to the next and continued making the last man searched pilot me to the next house to be searched. I must have searched at least 20 houses that night. I always threw guards around the house the first thing, then I would knock at the door and order them to open up. They would most always strike a light as soon as I knocked and I could see them through the window, getting their guns. I would tell them I was an army officer and that I had their house surrounded and to offer resistance meant certain death to them. This never failed to make them lay down their arms and open the door and submit quietly to the search; but they would all swear they knew nothing of any deserters or bounty jumpers. These bounty jumpers, as they were called, were fellows who would go where there was a good bounty of several hundred dollars offered to anyone who would enlist. These fellows would enlist, get the bounty and then desert; generally before they were regularly mustered into the U.S. Army; they would then change their names, go to another recruiting station, enlist again and do the same thing over again and again. They were harbored by the copperheads the same as deserters. They were more despicable than the deserters by far.

When it was getting almost daylight there was one more house I wished to search but going to it I would have to go by a still house. I was afraid my "battalion of braves" might get whiskey there and become unmanageable, as they were getting very tired and hungry and rather rebellious against discipline. They were wanting to commit some depredations which I would not allow, so I concluded to put off the search of this house for another raid. I felt beaten when I found out afterwards that this house I had failed to raid was filled with deserters and bounty jumpers at the time. It would have been the joy of my life to have led my braves against that gang, for there would have been something doing.[160]

The next night more than forty of these copperheads made a raid on the south side of the river with full intentions of getting me—in fact the whole object of the raid was to kill me as they had learned that I was the one who had led the raid on them the night before. I had anticipated this and had planned my defense. Our house was two stories high and the front door opened into a hall. There was a hall directly over this with a door opening directly over the lower front door. It had been the intention to build a veranda in front of this upper door but it had not yet been built. I was satisfied that the raiders would come to the front door to demand admittance. I told my father I was expecting the copperheads to be after me that night and I told him if they came to refuse to open the door and parry with them until the whole gang had time to gather in a body in front of the door; then I would open fire on their heads with my artillery

---

[160] This incident is referred to in a letter from "Q" to the *Parke County Republican*, 4 May 1864. The writer defends Durham's actions, stating he "ran all over the neighborhood searching houses," "in a community where the inhabitants had been in the habit of concealing [deserters]."

from the upper door. I stood watching all night at this upper door and I had it a little ajar so that I could open it instantly. My arsenal consisted of an army musket, a double-barreled shotgun loaded with buckshot, three Navies and my sword. I knew I could drop a half dozen or more of them and throw them in a stampede before they realized where the hail of lead was coming from. It is not often a fellow likes to have a mob after him when he knows they are anxious for his blood but I was really anxious for them to come after me that night for I despised a copperhead man worse than I did a snake and I knew I could stampede a hundred of those copperheads. Besides, I knew I could make several good copperheads that would never harm anyone again.

This gang that were coming to pay their respects to me that night had to pass by the house of old man Ley [sic], who was a radical Union man, and they concluded to stop and kill the old man before they tackled me. The old man was game and he stood behind his door and chopped them with a corn knife as they entered his house. He hacked several of them before he fell. They shot him six times and left him for dead but the old fellow finally got well. It was said he killed a couple of them with his corn knife and wounded several others. One of the gang, when he went to mount his horse to leave the Ley house, broke his saddle stirrup and in some way his gun was discharged and blew the whole top of his head off, killing him instantly. They then decided to take their dead and wounded home and recruit a larger gang and call on me the next night.[161] They were expecting a little trouble when they came to attend to my case and the experience they had at Ley's made them think it best to enlarge the gang. But early the next morning a message came with the information of the supposed murder of old man Ley and with a written request from Colonel Budd, the colonel of the Home Guards, ordering me to take command of the advance guard.[162]

I at once sent a runner to Russelville, 7 miles away, for some of the boys of my regiment who were home on veteran leave. I knew they would obey my orders and were as anxious to pay their respects to the copperheads as I was. Four of the boys came as fast as their horses could bring them. They were well mounted and had their army guns with them. We reported at once to Colonel Budd. He had a company of the Home Guards assembled and ready for action. The Colonel asked me to take command of the expedition and I accepted. I ordered Captain Burford, the captain of this home guard company, to follow with his company while I took my four veterans and went ahead as advance guards or scouts.[163] My father was determined to be in this campaign so I let him go with me and my veterans as a scout.

We went directly to a place called Hells Half Acre, where there was the worst nest of these copperheads in the state.[164] I captured every traitor I could find and turned them over to the home guard

[161] "Copperheads" or "Butternuts" in the area offered the excuse that the attack on Lay was in retaliation for Durham's search for deserters (*Parke County Republican*, 4 May 1864). George Lay, a citizen of Howard Township, Parke County, was assaulted by a group of twenty-five to thirty armed men. The group initially told Lay they were searching for stolen goods, and when he refused to open his door, the mob broke it open with a rail. Lay wounded one man with a corn-knife, but the group then fired a volley of ten or fifteen shots. Two bullets struck Lay, one in the groin and one in the chest. The party then fled the scene to nearby Fountain County IN. According to an Indianapolis newspaper account, one of the attackers placed a cocked pistol in his pocket, and while mounting his horse accidentally shot himself in the bowels, inflicting a mortal wound. Lay survived the attack (*Parke County Republican*, 20 April, 27 April, 4 May 1864; *Indianapolis Daily Journal*, 23 April, 28 April, 2 May 1864).

[162] Casper Budd of Waveland was commissioned colonel of the Parke County Regiment, Indiana Legion, in October 1862. He resigned in August 1864 (William H. H. Terrell, *Report of the Adjutant General of the State of Indiana*, vol. 3 [Indianapolis: Samuel. M. Douglass, 1866] 592. Apparently the sheriff of Parke County and a posse attempted to arrest Lay's attackers, but the "Copperheads" resisted and two deserters in their ranks were wounded. The local members of the Legion were then called out. As Durham indicates, Budd assembled his force the morning following the attack on Lay. A company of the Montgomery County Legion from Waveland commanded by Captain Buchanan acted in cooperation with Budd's troops (*Indianapolis Daily Journal*, 28 April, 2 May 1864).

[163] Possibly James Buford, a resident of Waveland and a first lieutenant in the Howard Guards, but more likely Captain Elijah N. Burford of Rockville, the commander of the Washington Guards, who was commissioned in September 1863 (Terrell, *Report of the Adjutant General*, vol. 3, 593–94; *Parke County Republican*, 25 November 1863).

company. I found nearly every one of them had been in the raid the night before when they tried to murder Ley and whose main object was to murder me. I found the saddle covered with blood and one stirrup gone. I had the other stirrup which matched the one on the saddle. I knew it was a nephew of the man who owned the saddle that rode it in the raid and was killed. They denied it bitterly, however. When I was approaching one house I saw about a dozen traitors running from the house. I ordered the boys to open fire on them and when the bullets began to tear up the ground around them we got to see some record-breaking running. When I searched the house I found drums and all the outfit for a military company. The son of the old fellow living here was the captain of an organized copperhead company and drilled it regularly. I could not capture the fellows that ran from this house as they hid in the hills. One thing that impressed me was the fear these cowardly copperhead traitors had of a regular soldier. They could tell one at a glance from the home guards or State Militia.

When I captured these fellows they appeared to be frightened and made no protest, but the moment I turned them over to the Home Guards, they cursed and frothed at the mouth and acted like they wanted to eat them up bodily. They seemed to have no fear of the State Militia. There was only one man I captured that offered any objection—this was the owner of the bloody saddle. His wife was a mink-eyed, sharp-nosed, thin-lipped woman with ivory white teeth. She came out to where I was and turned loose on me with her viper tongue. I have never seen anyone who could hold a light to her in profanity and vile language. She used the most profane profanity and

---

[164] Probably a reference to the "Devil's half acre" in Fountain County IN. Thomas Cunningham, one of the men charged in the attempted murder of Lay, was a resident of this area, and the party involved in the attack fled into Fountain County (*Parke County Republican*, 27 April 1864; *Indianapolis Daily Journal*, 2 May 1864).

the vilest of vile words I had ever heard. She said she never had expected to see the damned bluecoated curs about her house. I ordered her to go to the house and she defied me. I then ordered a couple of the veteran boys to fix bayonets and bring their guns to guard. I then ordered them to move forward and hang the she-copperhead on their bayonets and take her and pitch her into the house. The boys moved forward with the bayonets pointing at her body, but she glared at them defiantly until the points were within a foot of her body, then she turned and ran into the house. She saw the boys intended to obey my order. When we started to leave with her husband as a prisoner, I saw he was sulky and moved off too slowly to suit me, so I ordered him to hurry up. He ventured to inform me that he was a man who never hurried. I told him I often took hurrying spells and that I would give him a hurry-up lesson free of charge. I ordered a couple of the boys to put their bayonets to his stern and make him move. This was fun for the boys and they were anxious to obey such orders. It had the desired effect for I had never seen a man move with a finer "cornfield stride" than he did when the bayonets were close behind him.

That day I captured and turned over to the Home Guard more than twenty of these copperheads. These prisoners were all put in jail at Rockville. Their cases were continued by the courts from time to time and about the close of the war all the cases were dismissed. I think the mistake was made in trying to deal with them by civil law, instead of military law, and they should have been courtmartialed for treason. But the copperheads of Hells Half Acre were never so bold after this raid and I doubt if to this day the fellow citizens of Hells Half Acre have a very fond remembrance of me.[165]

After recruiting and reorganizing our regiment, we left Indianapolis on the morning of April 30, 1864, for New Orleans, La. The citizens of Indianapolis gave us a great banquet before we left and we were given another banquet by the citizens of Terre Haute, Ind., when we reached there. At Cairo, Illinois, we took a steamer down the Mississippi River and arrived at New Orleans on May 8th. On the 26th we took a train for Thibodaux [sic], La. This town is about forty miles west of New Orleans and located on La Fourche Bayou.[166] On June 6th my company was detached from the regiment and sent to Chucchorda Station on the New Orleans and Berwick Bay railroad, 60 miles west of New Orleans. Here we had a fearful time with mosquitoes as the station was surrounded with swamps. The gallinippers were so thick a fellow could hardly stir them with a stick. We built fires around our camp, thinking we could drive them away by smoking them but they did not seem to mind it while the smoke almost suffocated us. These gallinippers stood barefooted fully an inch high. They would bite a fellow through an army blanket and his clothes. Their bite was as attractive as the sting of a yellow jacket.

Here I decided that we were destined to stay idle and simply guard certain points until the war was over.[167] I knew it was over in the west and I had no hope of us being sent east. Such an inactive life did not appeal to me and as I was very anxious to get more education, I determined to resign, go home and enter school. My resignation was approved the 13th of June 1864 and I reached home

---

[165] The letter from "Q" to the *Parke County Republican* noted that 500 Legion members and others searched for the "cowardly assassins" of Mr. Lay. Apparently some members of the expedition acquired liquor and did "some very improper things" when confronted by the insolent Butternuts, but some arrests were made (*Parke County Republican*, 4 May 1864). One source indicates that seven or eight men were released on bail, two were held in the Rockville IN jail as they were unable to give bail, and another twenty or thirty were released due to a lack of evidence. Another source states that initially six men were arrested for the attack, but eight or ten men were later charged as well, including two deserters (*Indianapolis Daily Journal*, 2 May 1864; *Parke County Republican*, 20 April, 27 April, 4 May 1864).

[166] Chaplain A. S. Ames of the 11th wrote that Thibodeaux was fifty-five miles west of New Orleans. Unlike Durham's experiences, Ames described fine living in Thibodeaux, with a pleasant Gulf breeze and cool nights. Intoxication among the troops was rare, he noted, and sickness almost nonexistent. Nonetheless, he did admit that the Hoosiers were more anxious to strike a blow to end the war than enjoy "easy camp and guard duty" (*Indianapolis Daily Journal*, 22 July 1864).

June 24th.[168] I bitterly regretted that I had resigned when I learned that through the personal request of General Lew Wallace, the regiment was ordered east and sent to the Shenandoah Valley under General Phil Sheridan. The regiment was in one battle after I left and it was the only battle or skirmish they ever had that I was not in. This was the Battle of Cedar Creek, fought October 19, 1864, where Sheridan made his famous ride from Winchester.

---

[167] Other officers in the regiment apparently thought the same thing. A letter written by the regiment's surgeon at Thibodeaux LA on 26 June 1864 indicated that "There has been no fighting at this post, nor are we expecting any soon" (*Indianapolis Daily Journal,* 13 July 1864).

[168] Durham tendered his resignation as second lieutenant in a 1 June 1864 letter from Thibodeaux LA to the assistant adjutant general of the Department of the Gulf. He cited several reasons for his decision, including "Family being so afflicted and Business affairs in such a bad condition" due to his three-year absence that they demanded his "immediate personal attention." In addition, he noted that there were three officers with his company, and when the non-veterans were mustered out, Company G would have only thirty-five men. Finally, Durham noted that he had never been absent from his command without proper authority (Thomas Wise Durham compiled military service record, RG 94, National Archives and Records Administration, Washington, DC).

BIBLIOGRAPHY

Printed Primary Sources
BOOKS
Adams, Henry C. Jr. *Indiana at Vicksburg.* Indianapolis: Wm. B. Burford, 1911.
Beckwith, H. W. *History of Montgomery County.* Chicago: H. H. Hill and N. Iddings, 1881.
Billings, John D. *Hardtack and Coffee: The Unwritten Story of Army Life.* 1888. Reprint, Chicago: R.R. Donnelley & Sons Co., 1960.
Bowen, A. W.and Co. *History of Montgomery County Indiana.* 2 volumes. Indianapolis: A. W. Bowen and Co., 1913.
Brock, R. A., editor. *Southern Historical Society Papers.* 52 volumes. Richmond VA: By the Society, 1901.
Chapman Brothers. *Portrait and Biographical Record of Montgomery, Parke and Fountain Counties, Indiana.* Chicago: Chapman Bros., 1893.
Coons, John W. *Indiana at Shiloh.* Indianapolis: William B. Burford, 1904.
Cowen, Janet C. *Crawfordsville, Indiana Land Entries, 1820–1830.* Indianapolis: self published, 1985.
Evans, Clement A., editor. *Confederate Military History, Extended Edition.* 17 volumes. 1899. Reprint, Wilmington NC: Broadfoot Publishing Co., 1987–1989.
Grant, Ulysses S. *Personal Memoirs of U. S. Grant.* 2 volumes. New York: Charles L. Webster & Co., 1885.
Heitman, Francis B. *Historical Register and Dictionary of the United States Army.* 2 volumes. Washington, DC: Government Printing Office, 1903.
Hewett, Janet B., editor. *The Roster of Confederate Soldiers.* 16 volumes. Wilmington NC: Broadfoot Publishing Co., 1996.
———, editor. *Supplement to the Official Records of the Union and Confederate Armies.* 100 volumes. Wilmington NC: Broadfoot Publishing Co., 1994–2001.
Kennedy, Joseph C. G. *Population of the United States in 1860; Compiled from the Original Returns of the Eighth Census, under the direction of the Secretary of the Interior.* Washington, DC: Government Printing Office, 1864.
McIntosh, James T., editor. *The Papers of Jefferson Davis.* 10 vols. to date. Baton Rouge: Louisiana State University Press, 1981.
Moore, Frank. *The Rebellion Record.* 11 volumes. New York: G. P. Putnam and D. Van Nostrand, 1861–1868.
New York Adjutant General, *Annual Report of the Adjutant-General of the State of New York For the Year 1903.* 43 parts. Albany: Oliver A. Quayle, 1894–1906.
Patterson, Robert. *A Narrative of the Campaign in the Valley of the Shenandoah in 1861.* Philadelphia: John Campbell, 1865.

Scribner, Theodore T. *Indiana's Roll of Honor*. Indianapolis: A. D. Streight, 1866.

Stevenson, David. *Indiana's Roll of Honor*. Indianapolis: self published, 1864.

Terrell, William H. H. *Report of the Adjutant General of the State of Indiana*. 8 volumes. Indianapolis: Alexander H. Conner, W. R. Holloway and Samuel M. Douglass, 1865–1869.

US Adjutant General's Office. *Official Army Register of the Volunteer Force of the United States Army*. 8 volumes. Washington, DC: Adjutant General's Office, 1865.

US War Department. *The War of the Rebellion: A Compilation of the Official Records of the Union and Confederate Armies*. 128 volumes. Washington, DC: Government Printing Office, 1880–1901.

———. *Atlas to Accompany the Official Records of the Union and Confederate Armies*. Washington, DC: Government Printing Office, 1891–1895.

Wallace, Lew. *An Autobiography*. 2 volumes. New York: Harper and Bros., 1906.

Wise, Barton H. *The Life of Henry A. Wise of Virginia, 1806–1876*. New York: The Macmillan Co., 1899.

ARTICLES

Cunningham, S. A. "Col. William Houston Patterson." *Confederate Veteran*, vol. 13 (May 1905): 236.

McGinnis, George F. "Shiloh." In *War Papers Read Before the Indiana Commandery, Military Order of the Loyal Legion of the United States*. Indianapolis: By the Commandery, 1898: 1-41

Smith, Channing M. "General Turner Ashby." *Confederate Veteran*, vol. 32 (July 1924): 286.

Printed Secondary Sources
BOOKS

Allen, Stacy D. "'If He Had Less Rank': Lewis Wallace." In *Grant's Lieutenants: From Cairo to Vicksburg*. Edited by Steven E. Woodworth. Lawrence: University Press of Kansas, 2001. 63–89.

Bearss, Edwin Cole. *The Vicksburg Campaign*. 3 volumes. Dayton OH: Morningside House, 1985–1986.

Cooling, Benjamin Franklin. *Forts Henry and Donelson: The Key to the Confederate Heartland*. Knoxville: The University of Tennessee Press, 1987.

Daniel, Larry J. *Shiloh: The Battle That Changed the Civil War*. New York: Simon and Schuster, 1997.

Elting, John R., and Michael J. McAfee, editors. *Long Endure: The Civil War Period, 1852–1867.* Novato CA: Presidio Press, 1982.

Faust, Patricia L., editor. *Historical Times Illustrated Encyclopedia of the Civil War.* New York: Harper Collins Publishers, 1986.

Flexner, James Thomas. *George Washington: Anguish and Farewell, 1793–1799.* Boston: Little, Brown & Co., 1969.

————. *George Washington: The Forge of Experience, 1732–1775.* Boston: Little, Brown & Co., 1965.

Gaff, Alan D. *On Many A Bloody Field: Four Years in the Iron Brigade.* Bloomington: Indiana University Press, 1996.

Hinton, Richard J. *John Brown and his Men.* New York: Funk and Wagnalls Co., 1894.

Hunt, Roger D., and Jack R. Brown. *Brevet Brigadier Generals in Blue.* Gaithersburg MD: Olde Soldier Books, 1990.

Johnson, Robert U. and Clarence C. Buel, editors. *Battles and Leaders of the Civil War.* Volume 1. New York: Thomas Yoseloff, 1956.

McKee, Irving. *"Ben-Hur" Wallace: The Life of General Lew Wallace.* Berkeley: University of California Press, 1947.

Moe, Richard. *The Last Full Measure: The Life and Death of the First Minnesota Volunteers.* New York: Henry Holt and Co., 1993.

Morsberger, Robert E., and Katharine M. Morsberger. *Lew Wallace: Militant Romantic.* New York: McGraw-Hill, 1980.

Oates, Stephen B. *To Purge this Land with Blood: A Biography of John Brown.* Amherst: The University of Massachusetts Press, 1970.

Perry, Oran. *Indiana in the Mexican War.* Indianapolis: Adjutant General's Office, 1908.

Remini, Robert V. *Henry Clay: Statesman for the Union.* New York: W. W. Norton & Co, 1991.

Summers, Festus P. *The Baltimore and Ohio in the Civil War.* New York: G. P. Putnam's Sons, 1939.

Sword, Wiley. *Shiloh: Bloody April.* New York: William Morrow & Co., 1974.

Thornbrough, Emma Lou. *Indiana in the Civil War Era, 1850–1880.* Indianapolis: Indiana Historical Society, 1965.

Tredway, G. R. *Democratic Opposition to the Lincoln Administration in Indiana.* Indianapolis: Indiana Historical Bureau, 1973.

Troiani, Don, Earl J. Coates, and James L. Kochan. *Don Troiani's Soldiers in America, 1754–1865.* Mechanicsburg PA: Stackpole Books, 1998.

Villard, Oswald Garrison. *John Brown, 1800–1859: A Biography Fifty Years After.* New York: Alfred A. Knopf, 1943.

Warner, Ezra J. *Generals in Blue: Lives of the Union Commanders.* Baton Rouge: Louisiana State University Press, 1964.

———. *Generals in Gray: Lives of the Confederate Commanders.* Baton Rouge: Louisiana State University Press, 1959.

Welcher, Frank J. *The Union Army, 1861–1865.* 2 volumes. Bloomington: Indiana University Press, 1989 and 1993.

Winslow, Hattie Lou, and Joseph R. H. Moore. *Camp Morton, 1861–1865: Indianapolis Prison Camp.* Indianapolis: Indiana Historical Society, 1940.

Work Projects Administration. *Maryland: A Guide to the Old Line State.* New York: Oxford University Press, 1940.

ARTICLES

Castel, Albert, editor. "The War Album of Henry Dwight." *Civil War Times Illustrated* 19/2 (May 1980): 32–36 .

McAfee, Michael J. "Uniforms and History: The Seventh Regiment New York State Militia." *Military Images* 13/5 (March–April 1992): 30–31.

———. "Uniforms and History: 11th Regiment—Indiana Zouaves, 1861." *Military Images* 17/6 (May–June 1996): 35–36

O'Reilly, David. "The Dandy 7th." *Military Images* 20/5 (March–April, 1999): 32–35.

Treichel, James A. "Lew Wallace at Fort Donelson." *Indiana Magazine of History* 59/1 (March 1963): 3–18.

Volpe, Vernon L. "'Dispute Every Inch of Ground': Major General Lew Wallace Commands Cincinnati, September, 1862." *Indiana Magazine of History* 85/2 (June 1989): 138–50.

Wallace, Harold Lew. "Lew Wallace's March to Shiloh Revisited." *Indiana Magazine of History* 59/1 (March 1963): 19–30.

NEWSPAPERS

Crawfordsville (IN) *Review*
Crawfordsville (IN) *Weekly Review*
Harper's Weekly
Indianapolis (IN) *Daily Journal.*
Ladoga (IN) *Ruralist*
National Tribune
New York Times
Parke County (IN) *Republican*

National Archives and Records Administration Census and Military Records, Washington, DC

Compiled Service Records of Confederate Soldiers Who Served in Organizations From the State of Georgia. Record group 109. Microcopy 266. Roll 443.

Eighth Census of the United States, 1860. Population Schedules for Montgomery County IN. Microcopy 653. Roll 283.

Thomas Wise Durham compiled military service record. Record group 94.

Thomas Wise Durham pension record. Record group 15.

Franklin Gill pension record. Record group 15.

William Rockwell pension record. Record group 15.

Other Manuscript Material

11th Indiana File. Vicksburg National Military Park Library.

Letter from Lew Wallace to Susan Wallace. 5 October 1861. Copy in files of Ben Hur Museum (Lew Wallace Study), Crawfordsville IN.

Indianapolis News articles in the *Scrapbook of Articles on World War I and Civil War Reunions and Obituaries of Crawfordsville Residents, 1909–1919.* Crawfordsville (IN) Public Library.

Personal correspondence with Dr. Earl J. Hess. Harrogate TN, 23 January 2000.

INDEX